HOW TO GROW

YOUR MONEY

WITHOUT WRECKING

THE EARTH

THE **ETHICAL** INVESTOR'S HANDBOOK

MORTEN STRANGE

Marshall Cavendish
Business

Published in 2018 by Marshall Cavendish Business
An imprint of Marshall Cavendish International

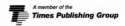
A member of the
Times Publishing Group

Other Marshall Cavendish Offices:
Marshall Cavendish Corporation. 99 White Plains Road, Tarrytown NY 10591–9001, USA • Marshall Cavendish International (Thailand) Co Ltd. 253 Asoke, 12th Flr, Sukhumvit 21 Road, Klongtoey Nua, Wattana, Bangkok 10110, Thailand • Marshall Cavendish (Malaysia) Sdn Bhd, Times Subang, Lot 46, Subang Hi-Tech Industrial Park, Batu Tiga, 40000 Shah Alam, Selangor Darul Ehsan, Malaysia.

Marshall Cavendish is a trademark of Times Publishing Limited

National Library Board, Singapore Cataloguing-in-Publication Data

Name(s): Strange, Morten.
Title: The Ethical Investor's Handbook: How to grow your money without wrecking the earth / Morten Strange.
Description: First edition. | Singapore: Marshall Cavendish Business, [2018]
Identifier(s): OCN 1050347308 | ISBN 978-981-4828-28-4 (paperback)
Subject(s): LCSH: Finance, Personal. | Finance, Personal–Moral and ethical aspects. | Investments. | Investments–Moral and ethical aspects. | Social responsibility of business.
Classification: DDC 332.024–dc23

Printed in Singapore

Contents

Where did all the animals go?
But this is nothing new – or is it?
A new normal
Plastic, plastic everywhere
Global warming
Overpopulation

The debt trap
The end of history?
Monetary weapons of mass (environmental) destruction
Interesting rates
Shortage or oversupply?
What will happen to the debt?

All we need is... more natural capital
Conserve your personal capital
What is nature worth?
Do we care?
Crooked accounting
Running in circles

Foreword

I was born with a deep fascination and love for nature and wildlife, and have been involved in nature conservation all my life. During my life, I have seen the conservation movement grow tremendously in size and scope and influence; awareness amongst the public and increasingly decision makers in governments and the private sector is greater than ever; the science about the problems, the consequences and the solution is also clearer than ever.

And yet, in spite of our many new initiatives and achievements, we are in the midst of a shocking decline in biodiversity. Loss of tropical rainforest is accelerating, not slowing down. The climate is destabilising. In fact, degradation of our natural world has begun to affect the very global ecological balance that we all depend on, with dangerous consequences for all life on Earth, including our own. It is time that we step back and consider why this is so. It is necessary that we think outside of the box and consider what is driving this deterioration.

At the 2018 WWF Global Conference in Colombia we focused on how we galvanise the world to commit to a new ambitious "Global Deal for Nature", the way it was committed to in Paris for climate. For this to happen we discussed the need to develop a new compelling narrative about the value of nature to us, our well-being, health, happiness and prosperity. A narrative that, alongside the crucially important ethical argument of respect and coexistence with nature, also highlights the benefits that nature provides to us, and the dangerous consequences if natural systems collapse. We need to advocate for more ambitious targets, more serious commitment to implementation and greater integration between nature, climate and sustainable development. We left that Conference inspired and energised but also still deeply concerned about the crisis the planet and our society face.

I know that Morten Strange shares this sense of concern and urgency. We stamped into each other a long time ago when we both attended the 1994 inaugural BirdLife International conference in Rosenheim, Germany. I worked at the time in a national organisation in Italy, LIPU, and Morten represented the counterpart in Denmark, DOF. We undoubtedly share the same genuine passion for our amazing, magnificent, inspiring natural world.

Morten left the NGO world a couple of years later in order to try to make an impact in the private sector, working on nature awareness-building, most recently as a financial analyst with a keen interest in economics, personal finance and ethical capital allocation. And I ended up leading WWF International, a globally distributed organisation with an holistic approach to solving today's ecological crisis and building a "future where people and nature live in harmony". WWF believes in an approach based on both delivering concrete conservation results on the field through protecting species and natural places, but also influencing the key drivers of nature loss from food production to financial flows, markets and governance.

To find solutions to our broken relationship with the natural world, we need everyone involved; in this book Morten has taken it upon himself to scrutinise these issues mainly from a financial and monetary point of view. While I might not agree with every statement Morten makes in this book, his work is a thought-provoking guide to being an ethical investor with much to be learned from in order to achieve the much-needed shift to ensure a future for our natural world and our own civilisation.

Dr Marco Lambertini
Director General
WWF International

Preface

"I cannot invest the way I want the world to be.
I have to invest the way the world is."

— JIM ROGERS

The famous Singapore-based American businessman wrote this in an invitation to the World Wealth Creation Conference in Singapore in November 2017. For what it is worth, I concur. All investors involved with the allocation of capital grapple with these issues – both institutional professionals as well as small retail investors trying to get a return on their modest savings. We want the world to be a certain way, to be nice; but we also want the best possible return on our investments. On one hand we want to be well-off; but on the other we don't want to do harm to others or to nature; we don't really want to wreck the earth.

Is it possible to invest in an ethical manner and still generate a good return on your capital? Yes, I think it is. In fact I have proven it myself. As I will explain later, in ethics there is no one-size-fits-all. We each have slightly different standards and priorities. But having said that, I also believe that there are some universal values that bind us together; at the bottom of our hearts most people know what it means to be a decent human being.

Not only is it possible to invest ethically and still come out ahead, there are many indications that investing with a conscience will in fact give you a leg up in the battle for yield. Like Jim Rogers, we should face reality for what it is. I don't recommend that you put on rose-tinted glasses and throw your hard-earned cash at some do-gooder start-up that promises to save the earth but is unlikely to ever get off the ground. When you are rich enough to go into social impact investing, by all means do so. In the meantime, consider carefully how you put your money to work. There are many moving parts to watch and many criteria and financial concepts and instruments that you need to be familiar with.

In this book I will cover what you need to know to invest ethically and still do well. "Ethics" is many things, but I think that we can all agree that we need to take care of the earth we live on, so that will be my main concern. I will explain why it is imperative that we start to think seriously about our environment and what is happening to it. And then I will show you how you can position yourself, learn from the best and structure your asset allocation across the sectors that are likely to benefit from the economic disruptions ahead.

The monetary references here are mainly in $, meaning US$. Where I refer to Singapore dollars I will make that clear with S$. One US$ is currently about S$1.35. In this day and age, most of my statements are easily checked online, so I don't cite every single piece of information I provide; this is not a scholarly work anyway. But where my assertions might be controversial and contested, or where I quote directly from others, I have included the source.

In December 2015 I met with two executives at the Marshall Cavendish offices in Singapore. I was pitching my book, *Be Financially Free*, and in general they liked the manuscript, but one of them said: "Most of the content is good, but I find the section about the environment and ethical investing a bit 'preachy'. I think that in general readers don't care so much for this; most people just want to get rich quick." Well, as it turned out, the editor put in charge of making a book out of my files was Justin Lau, and Justin happened to like the "preachy" parts! When the book appeared in June 2016, all the environmental stuff was there; in fact Justin helped rewrite some of it, so that it came out even clearer and stronger.

Be Financially Free didn't quite make it to the New York Times bestseller list, but it did fairly well and was reprinted in 2017; Domain Publishing Company in Taiwan issued a Chinese edition. In 2018, the English edition was reprinted again, and that year, in March, managing editor Melvin Neo of Marshall Cavendish wrote me an email and suggested that we did a follow-up to *Be Financially Free* together, this time focusing mainly on ethical investing issues! Sometimes life is funny that way, isn't it? I agreed, and the result is the book you are holding now. I want to thank Marshall Cavendish and all their staff for the trust and support they have shown me throughout these last few years.

At first I was a bit apprehensive about the new project. Like Jim Rogers and many others, I have the general impression that most investors are mainly concerned about ROI (return on investment) and yield; other priorities take a back seat. That is my notion from the financial media, from investors I meet and from financial events I attend. So would anyone care, would anyone actually buy this book? There are already several books out there on these matters; most are called something with SRI (Socially Responsible Investing) – I will go into that in more detail later. But then I thought some more about it. And three factors made me write this book:

1. Sometimes public sentiment changes fast; and sentiment is changing very fast right now. In 2015, ethical considerations were at the fringes of the investment community; today they are almost mainstream, and soon I predict they will be a major factor for both institutional and retail investors. Virtually every major company has an ESG (Environmental, Social and Governance) policy and/or an environmental department. How much of that is just "green-washing" we will look at later, but environmental and ethical issues are here to stay. And investors had better pay attention to them.

2. Most people don't want to be unethical; most people feel better when they do the right thing. And you *can* make money without wrecking the earth and without compromising your other values of decency and civility. But it helps to study how. There are concepts and tools and methods that you need to learn and to apply. I love to deal with those and to share my insights with others; that is my main interest and passion. So this book is a hands-on manual that you can use in your training.

3. And finally, this is *my* version of events. Although I draw heavily on financial experts and other authoritative sources, I want to show – using my own experiences – that ethical investing is not only important, but also lucrative. I am not an academic or a theorist; I have actually been there and done that. I have toiled out in the freezing cold and the scorching heat on oil rigs, I have worked for a bird conservation society, I have run my own company. I bought my first financial securities when I was 18 years old and crude oil was $3 a barrel (not $75); gold was $38 per ounce (not $1,200). Besides, although much of the material in this book is universal in nature and can apply to all jurisdictions globally, this is also the first book on the subject with a Singaporean/Asian bias; after all, some three billion people live in this region and we must find our own way.

Together with *Be Financially Free*, this book will enable you to get the most out of your money, and to live in freedom and in harmony with your surroundings.

Morten Strange
Singapore
July 2018

1

What in the World Is Wrong?

"Ultimately, we are the endangered species."
— PATRICK LEAHY

Where did all the animals go?

Why do we have to be concerned for the world? There are lots of reasons, but let me just provide you with a few examples to give you an idea of the scope of the problem.

In June 1971 I visited the Norwegian island of Runde, off the west coast, just south of Ålesund. It is the southern-most location for breeding seabirds in Norway. There were hundreds of thousands of them at the time; I have the photographs I took that year to prove it. They landed on the steep cliffs dropping into the Atlantic Ocean and nested on the narrow ledges in dense colonies.

My naturalist Singaporean wife has never experienced this spectacle – the Atlantic bird cliffs – so this year, 2018, some 47 years later, I did some research for a possible trip out there. The island of Runde is still there – in fact there is a bridge connecting it to the mainland now, so you can drive all the way. Very convenient. But the birds are gone. I checked out one of the local websites and found that compared to the 1970s Runde now has just a few birds, mainly one species, the Atlantic Puffin. Most of the others have been decimated. The Kittiwake, a small gull, used to appear here, with 100,000–200,000 breeding pairs; today there are just a few, and some years none breed successfully. The Guillemot: 10,000 pairs before, today around 20. The Razorbill, Black Guillemot, Fulmar, Shag, Arctic Tern? Just "a few" left.

What happened? According to the report "Silent Spring in the Bird Mountains" (in reference to Rachel Carson's famous 1962 book *Silent Spring* about the pesticide crisis), sea temperatures in the area have gone up by 1.5°C, causing oceanic plankton to move north to colder waters. Over-fishing of herring and other commercial species has emptied out most of the rest of the fish. The seabirds on Runde cannot find food for their young and are gradually dying out. The reporter couldn't help including a dig at the Norwegian oil industry: "The oil, Norway's national wealth, strikes back. We are about to lose our natural heritage because the oil gets burned and causes global warming."[1]

This is what has happened to the natural world in just the last few decades, in my lifetime. In Denmark, where I grew up, a survey in 2018 found that 2.9 million birds have disappeared from the country in the past 40 years, mainly due to the use of more intensive farming methods.[2] In France, one-third of the bird population died out between 2003 and 2018, according to a survey by the French National Centre for Scientific Research; the authors called the event an "environmental catastrophe". The birds starved to death, their food sources wiped out by pesticide use.[3] For Europe as a whole, some 500 million birds disappeared between 1984 and 2014.[4] If intensive agriculture and pesticides don't get the birds, hunting will. Some 25 million birds are killed by illegal hunting in countries around the Mediterranean region each year.[5] You would think that an organised society like Germany would be able to protect its biodiversity, yet only 4% of land in Germany is conserved as nature reserves; legal as well as illegal hunting of animals is rampant, as is illegal trading in all sorts of exotic animals such as reptiles, birds and even insects.[6]

I mention these cases to show that the loss of species and sheer animal numbers is not only a Third World problem. Of course, the degradation of habitats and animal life is particularly critical in the tropics; these regions are the lungs of the world and a treasure trove of biodiversity. When I came to Asia in 1980 and started working on the oil rigs in Indonesia, Sumatra and Kalimantan (Indonesia's part of Borneo) were still largely covered in dense virgin rainforest. Today there are just a few protected areas and fragmented forest patches left. Bird numbers have been decimated, and not just by habitat loss; studies by BirdLife International have identified a crisis in Indonesia, where many species are being captured for the unbridled trade in caged songbirds.[7]

In the last 50 years, some 90% of the large fish stocks have been taken out of the oceans. We simply gobbled up the sea; the fish have been replaced with an infestation of jellyfish or just emptiness.

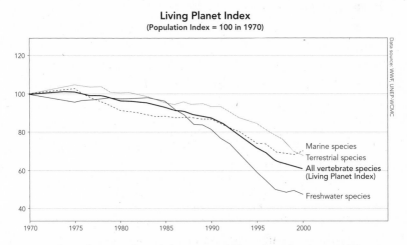

Living Planet Index
(Population Index = 100 in 1970)

Data source: WWF, UNEP-WCMC

Since I got my driver's licence in 1970 we have lost some 40% of our animals (not species, individuals) according to the Living Planet Index compiled by the WWF and others.

In terms of species richness, the IUCN (International Union for Conservation of Nature) calculates the status of our flora and fauna regularly. The last time I checked, there were 41,415 species that the organisation evaluates; out of those, 16,306 are facing global extinction; 25% of mammals, 13% of birds, 33% of amphibians and 70% of plants are endangered; 785 species are recorded as already extinct; another 65 survive only in captivity or in cultivation.[8]

The reasons for all this vary greatly from region to region and country to country, but to quote the Living Planet survey again, these are the reasons why we are seeing such a dramatic decline in wildlife globally:

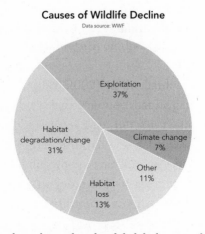

Causes of Wildlife Decline
Data source: WWF

Exploitation 37%

Habitat degradation/change 31%

Climate change 7%

Other 11%

Habitat loss 13%

This chart shows that the global decline in wildlife is our fault entirely. We deprive the animals of a home, we hunt and capture and/or eat the others. Especially on oceanic islands, introduced species such as rats and cats have caused havoc; climate change adds to the problem.

In the developed world, the situation is bad; but in the Third World, it is catastrophic. A 2016 report published in the journal *Royal Society Open Science* concluded that "hundreds of mammal species – from chimpanzees to hippos to bats – are being eaten into extinction by people". The author, Professor David Macdonald at the University of Oxford, said when the report was published: "There are a plenty of bad things affecting wildlife around the world and habitat loss and degradation are clearly at the fore-front, but among the other things is the seemingly colossal impact of bushmeat hunting. You might rejoice at having some habitat remaining, say a pristine forest, but if is hunted out to become an empty larder, it is a pyrrhic victory." He added: "The number of hunters involved has gone up, and the penetration of road networks into the remotest places is such that there is no refuge left. So it becomes commercially possible to make a trade out of something that was once just a rabbit for the pot. In places like Cameroon, where I have worked, you see flotillas of taxis early in the morning going out to very remote areas and being loaded up with the (bushmeat) catch and taken back to towns."[9]

In Southeast Asia, a study in 2016 published in *Conservation Biology* found evidence that animal populations have declined sharply at multiple sites across the region since 1980, with many species now completely wiped out in substantial portions of their former ranges. The report concluded: "Tropical Southeast Asia (Northeast India, Indochina, Sundaland, Philippines) is experiencing a wildlife crisis. Large areas of natural forest across the region are nearly devoid of large animals, except for a few hunting-tolerant species. Previous estimates have held that only one percent of the land area in tropical Asia still supports an intact fauna of mammals, but in reality the situation is far worse." The authors found that while most conservation organisations focus on the international wildlife trade, local hunting is overlooked because most of the animals are consumed and kept as pets locally. With urban affluence stoking demand for wildlife-derived medicinal products, and the advent of modern hunting techniques, "hunting is by far the most severe immediate threat to the survival of Southeast Asia's endangered vertebrates".[10]

But this is nothing new – or is it?

So we have a natural world in rapid decline. But it has always been this way, hasn't it? And does it even matter? We are all better off and richer than ever, aren't we? What's the big deal?

Correct; since humans first travelled out of Africa and started invading the world some 60,000 years ago, we have altered the world and shaped it into something that fits us better. When I went to school, we were taught that at first humans were primitive and lived in caves or travelled around like nomads, living off the land. But then they invented agriculture and things got much better. In more recent years I have seen this version of events challenged.

Clive Ponting (2007), for instance, makes the case that the early Stone Age hunter-and-gatherers were actually not too badly off. There was plenty of prey to hunt and nutritious food plants to pick, and in general they probably didn't work very hard to survive. When people started cultivating the land, which happened in several places simultaneously around 12,000 BC, they gradually got worse off, not better! Yes, the communities could get larger, but people had to work much harder growing crops. Harvests were uncertain; storage of food over the seasons was difficult; living in close proximity to domesticated animals brought with it many new diseases. However, it was too late to go back to the old way of life; the land could no longer support the growing human population in a natural way. A long epoch of perpetual poverty and general misery followed; ironically the Black Death in Europe in the mid-1300s eased the population pressure on the land and made life a bit more tolerable for the survivors. Otherwise, it wasn't until the early modern period (starting during the 1600s) and then the Industrial Revolution (starting around 1760) that conditions started to improve. Even then, Ponting writes, "there is no evidence of any improvement in the living standards of the bulk of the population until the late 1840s at the earliest".

Sure, people have always been exterminating animals. When Asians first crossed the Bering land bridge into North America some 20,000 years ago and started colonising that empty continent (empty of people, but full of animals), the first thing they did was take out all the Pleistocene megafauna such as the Woolly Mammoth and other mastodons, the Sabre-toothed Tiger, a giant armadillo species, the Short-faced Bear, American Cheetah, Ground Sloth, camels, horses, etc. Later, when the European settlers arrived, they hunted down the rest, virtually emptying out the American West of fur-bearing animals. The tale of the Passenger Pigeon (*Ectopistes migratorius*) is well known: up until the 19th century it was the most numerous bird in North America, numbering between 3 and 5 billion (not million, *billion*) individuals. Flocks darkened the sky for days when they flew over. And yet, the last Passenger Pigeon died in captivity in 1914. If people can bring a bird that numerous to extinction, they can exterminate anything.

Everywhere people went, they first took out most of the megafauna and then the rest of the little stuff. New Zealand was one of the last major places on Earth to be colonised by man; the early Polynesian settlers arrived around 1300 and immediately did away with all the moas (a family of huge flightless birds) and many of the other indigenous animals. Since then, almost half of the original vertebrate species on New Zealand have gone extinct, and many of the rest are barely clinging on. What has replaced these native species? Introduced Blackbirds and Goldfinches that the British settlers released to remind them of home!

So what is different now? The difference with modern man is that we don't just take out the large animals, we remove the whole ecosystem. We cut the rainforest and turn it into barren grasslands; we dynamite the coral reefs; we bulldoze the landscape and build villages and urban sprawl. There is no nature left; everything goes, including insects and fungi and bacteria. Once you remove a tropical rainforest and the rains wash out the sandy soils, it can never grow back; only grasses, invasive scrubs and heavily fertilised monoculture crops can replace it. Considering all this, the current rate of species extinction in historical terms is thousands of times the natural so-called "background" rate of extinction.

Already in 1979, Norman Myers dealt with this crisis in his book *The Sinking Ark*. Industrial pollution can be cleaned up, according to Myers, but species extinctions are final and constitute an irreversible impoverishment of life on Earth. More recently, in *A New Green History of the World* (2007), Clive Ponting claimed that "half of all the world's existing species will be extinct by 2100", adding that "the economic forces promoting habitat destruction and climate change will be the driving force" behind species extinction. In the next chapter we will take a look at some of the economic forces Ponting talks about. I believe that they are important if you want to understand what is going on and position yourself going forward.

A new normal

The loss of biodiversity in the name of development appears to be inevitable and irreversible. And we don't know yet what the full consequences of this will be. I agree with the experts who claim that all species are important, and that we should preserve and protect each one of them; that we should err on the side of caution and keep our natural world intact at all cost to avoid a collapse of first the environment and ultimately our social cohesion.

But I also understand the argument from many in the Third World, that Europe ruined their own environment (let's face it, how much authentic, virgin forest and habitat is left there?), they got rich that way, and now they tell others to stay the way they are. I get that. So while we grapple with the outcome of our biodiversity crisis, by all means let us make the best of what we have left.

You can still have some nature after the bulldozers and the builders leave, after the rainforest has been turned into an urban park. In the case of Denmark, yes, there are fewer birds now than when I was a kid there. But some animals have also moved in. Some adaptable species will do that if you leave them alone. They will re-colonise even an urbanised area if you give them a chance. There are more eagles in Denmark now, and even some megafauna like moose and wolves have started to turn up, after hundreds of years of absence. Some of the other changes in the fauna and flora are less welcome; introduced species like the American Mink (escaped from mink farms), Racoon Dog, Muntjak Deer and a host of other animals and plants are considered invasive, as they do damage to native species and authentic ecosystems.

In Singapore, we have seen new populations of large animals like the Smooth-coated Otter and Wild Boar turn up recently – to the joy of many, but also to the consternation of a few, who worry about human-animal conflicts. In the same period, meanwhile, our rainforest birds have been decimated in numbers; many are close to local extinction, some are probably gone already. Altogether, Singapore has lost some 70 bird species, mainly rainforest special-ists, since records began in the early 19th century.[11]

But even in view of all this, the question remains: Do we need all these other animals? Does it matter that we lose some biodiver-sity? I will get back to that a bit later, when we look at the wider financial and economic implications of the biodiversity decline. For now, let us just establish that nature is collapsing around us. There are fewer different species, and the ones remaining – or at least all those that can't adapt to urban life – are crashing in numbers.

But there is one thing we have much more of now, and that is garbage.

Plastic, plastic everywhere

What happened to all the forests we cut, and all the coal and crude oil we sucked out of the ground since the 18th century? Most of it was burned, filling up the atmosphere with carbon dioxide (CO_2) in the process; and the rest was turned into garbage, especially plastic garbage. The problem is that unlike the old garbage – wood, paper, and even cast iron – plastic does not go away.

As we will see later, waste management is one of the great growth industries of our time! Do we dump the stuff into landfills? Do we burn it? How much can be recycled? That is the general management part. But in the case of plastic, much of it never even makes it to the dump. Less than 10% of plastic bottles are recycled. Natural degrading takes at least 450 years, under some circumstances twice that or longer.

I used to go to the Indonesian island of Bali regularly during the 1980s and into the 1990s; it was an amazingly beautiful place. I worked on a project to conserve the endemic Bali Starling (*Leucopsar rothschildi*) inside the Bali Barat National Park in the northwest of the island; and I travelled all over the island and nearby Nusa Penida to photograph birds. By the way, that project – protecting the Bali Starling – didn't work out; when I started, there were hundreds of those snow-white starlings, and you could see flocks of them come down from the hills to roosting sites along the coast every night. Today that species is extinct in the wild. The poachers took them all out. Only a handful of captive-bred re-introduced individuals are left in the national park.

I went back to Bali a few years ago and was shocked. The 20-minute drive from the airport to our bungalow took two hours due to gridlock traffic. The stunning Kuta Beach – a former white-sand surfer-dude and bikini-chick haven – was covered in plastic and garbage. North of Sanur Beach, on the east coast of the island, a river was pouring a toxic mixture of thick brown sewage and pollutants from tanneries straight into the ocean; the stench was overwhelming. The picturesque river running through the village of Ubud up in the hills appeared to be two-thirds water and one-third plastic bags. A video of a diver swimming across a coral reef near Nusa Penida in an ocean of garbage – literally – went viral. See if you can still catch it and you will understand what I am talking about.[12] We are starting to recognise the catastrophic overuse of wrapping material and the reckless discharging of waste for what it is: a crime against the earth.

Lots of solutions have been offered to the plastic menace. We can recycle more; we can substitute it with biodegradable packaging materials; we can scoop the stuff out of the ocean when it gets that far. And yet, nothing really seems to be done. In March 2018, the BBC could report that the famous "Great Pacific Garbage Patch" is not shrinking but growing! It is now twice the size of France and contains some 80,000 tons of mainly plastic waste, but also old fishing nets, nylon ropes and other stuff lethal to marine life. Although most of the garbage originates from the rivers of Asia, this largest patch is located between Hawaii and California. There are several more of these patches in the Atlantic, Indian and Pacific oceans, mainly where the trade winds and associated currents whirl the stuff together. The study reported by BBC found

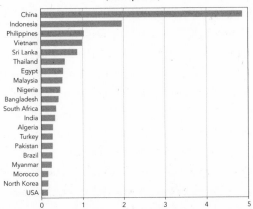

Plastic Debris Contributed to Oceans in 2010
(billion pounds)

As this figure show, Asia – especially China, and Indonesia up there as well – is responsible for most of the plastic polluting the oceans.

that based on observations over a three-year period, plastic pollution is increasing exponentially and "is expected to treble between 2015 and 2025".[13] Some of the plastic breaks down into so-called microplastics that are very difficult to detect when they enter the oceanic food chain and contaminate plankton, birds, fish – and eventually humans.

Global warming

Let me add to this cheerful chapter a little bit about global warming – something that has really transformed our attitude to the environment and galvanised the conservation movement. It will take on significant importance later on, when we consider how investors should position themselves in our new economy.

When I went to school in the 1960s, we were taught that it was getting colder, that the earth was about to enter a new ice age. "Climatologists generally accept the fact that the earth's climate is tending towards an ice age of some sort, and that a new North American ice sheet may be forming" – so it says in a book I still own published by the University of Alaska, quoting from a report in *Nature* in March 1973.[14]

I actually visited Alaska the year after that, in 1974. I spent the whole summer there and yes, it was indeed pretty cold. I was at Barrow – at 71° North the most northerly village in the United States – from mid-June to mid-July. That was supposed to be summer, but by the time I left, I still couldn't see any open water in the Beaufort Sea; the rugged sea ice came all the way up to the shoreline. When I hiked around the tundra fields to photograph birds, the permafrost was so thick that when I wanted to set up camp for the "night" (there was no night, of course – the sun never set!), I never could insert my tent pegs more than a few centimetres into the ground. Today I hear there is open water around Barrow for most of the year, and the permafrost is turning into mush in the summers.

The ice age never came as we were told it would, but global warming sure did. More than any other nature conservation issue, this has helped grab the headlines, finally. Rachel Carson's *Silent Spring* in 1962 came and went; the *Limits to Growth* report in 1972 didn't make us change our ways; nor did the Brundtland Commission report on sustainable development in 1987. The Earth Summit in Rio in 1992 made no difference – actually that was the same period when consumption and associated waste and pollution exploded, in China and other emerging markets.

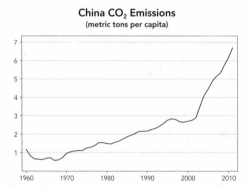

China CO$_2$ Emissions
(metric tons per capita)

The Earth Summit took place in Rio de Janeiro in 1992. That was also about the time when pollution and CO$_2$ release from China started to skyrocket.

In a study reported in *The Conversation* in 2017, Professor Michael Howe with Griffith University set out to investigate what happened after that ground-breaking summit in 1992 when 170 countries agreed to move into sustainable development, protect biodiversity and stop deforestation and global warming. He found that nothing happened. Forest and biodiversity loss, greenhouse gas emissions and general environmental deterioration continued at about the same pace as they had since the 1970s. The study concluded that in spite of "humanity fast approaching several environmental tipping points", policies hadn't changed, mainly because of "the basic problem that environmentally damaging activities are financially rewarded".[15]

However, the issue of global warming could change that. This topic has at long last put the state of our environment high on the agenda. When I was a kid, we didn't hear much about the environment; today not a day goes by that pollution and global warming issues are not out there in the debate. Every school kid around the world knows about this now, that the earth is warming and that it is our fault, and that the consequences will be dire for many.

There are contrarian observers who point out that global warming may in fact be good for certain regions. For instance, some agricultural activities can move north. That might be so, but at the moment I just cannot think of areas that would benefit much from higher temperatures. The cold north? You would think that a little warming there would be alright; but I am not so sure. To go back to Alaska, that state has been hit hard; in general, warming in the northern states has been above the global average. When I was last there in 2015, my friend's estate just north of Fairbanks had big sink-holes around the place; his neighbour's house was abandoned and about to collapse. The permafrost was melting and turning into unstable soft matter. Around the west and north coast of the state, melting permafrost and coastal erosion are wreaking havoc on Inupiat and Athabascan villages. "More than 30 Native villages are either in the process of or in need of relocating their entire village" – so writes the American EPA (Environmental Protection Agency); damage to highways and airstrips, forest fires and pest infestations are other challenging consequences of global warming.[16]

It is a bit of a paradox that next to Alaska it is the state of Louisiana that has been hardest hit by climate change in America. The two are in opposite corners of the continent and both have benefited from the extraction of coal, oil and minerals; they are also traditionally "red" states where conservative Republican

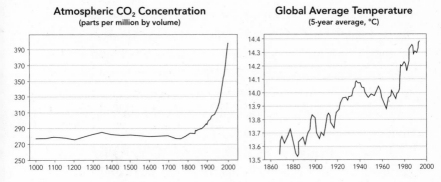

These charts show how atmospheric CO_2 concentration increased after the Industrial Revolution, correlating positively with rising global temperatures.

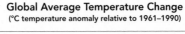

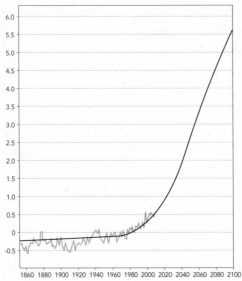

This is one of the many projections out there of how global air temperatures may rise in the future.

values rule. Some one-third of the members of the US Congress are climate sceptics. If you talk to the miners and the oil field workers in Alaska, they will acknowledge that the climate is getting warmer. This is hard to deny when your house is falling apart. But they will then tell you right away that this has nothing to do with them; these are natural changes in the weather patterns, most likely caused by regular astronomical cycles and solar activity out of our control.

I respect that view; we don't all have to think alike. What's most important is that we take care of the earth and conserve what is left; our reasoning or motives are less important. The thing about the global warming and climate change debate is that it finally makes nature protection seem urgent. Collectively it is my general observation that we don't really care so much for the little animals; a new smartphone will always be more important to us. But we do care if our house gets flooded or if it burns down. And flooding is happening right now from New York down to Miami in Florida, where people can no longer get flood insurance. In California, houses are burning down by the hundreds every year, and agriculture is ravaged by heat waves and drought. It seems that tragedies like these are needed before we take action.

It is great that the world is finally waking up to see the environmental crisis for what it is: existential. But it is also pretty clear that whatever we do now will help, but it will be too little too late. The Kyoto Protocol in 1997, the Paris climate accord in 2015 – these were wonderful achievements, but we must not kid ourselves that these agreements will fix all our problems. They will not.

Global warming is here to stay – and accelerate – and little will be done to change it. Naomi Klein put out a really powerful book in 2014, *This Changes Everything*, where she takes the climate change deniers to task; it is a great read, and I will be referring to it in more detail later. But in reality nothing has changed; the book was written before the American public elected the greatest climate denier of all to lead them forward.

Clive Ponting (2007) points out how positive feedback loops from methane – a powerful greenhouse gas (GHG) – released when the vast Arctic tundra melts, and from warming oceans exposed to the sun as the polar ice cap disappears, will accelerate the warming process. As the earth warms, soils will release more GHGs; the warmer oceans will absorb less CO_2. Ponting points to the melting glaciers, especially in Greenland, and writes: "Continued melting on this scale would raise sea levels very rapidly – possibly by five metres in a century." He thinks we are underestimating the rises in temperatures: "The IPCC's worst-case estimate in 2007 was a rise of 6.4°C by 2100, which most observers agree would be catastrophic for the world, may also be too low." Referring to the positive feedback loops, Ponting concludes that at the end of the century, "the best available estimate is that global temperatures would, on average, be about 10°C warmer than they are now".

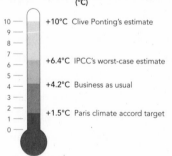

Increase in Global Temperature by 2100 (°C)

10 —
9 —
8 —
7 —
6 —
5 —
4 —
3 —
2 —
1 —
0 —

+10°C Clive Ponting's estimate

+6.4°C IPCC's worst-case estimate

+4.2°C Business as usual

+1.5°C Paris climate accord target

So far, global temperature increase has been in the order of 0.8°C since industrialisation. What will an increase of 10°C bring, or even 4.2°C?

Overpopulation

And finally there is our biggest existential emergency of all. When ecosystems break down and terrestrial, oceanic and atmospheric pollution is choking us, it really comes down to one factor: There are too many of us; the earth simply cannot cope. In a 2017 survey of Nobel Prize winners on the gravest threats to humanity, the single most important threat identified, by 34% of the participants, was overpopulation and climate change.[17]

The enormous oversupply of people has lead to a dramatic drop in the value of each one of us. Professor Kevin Bales with the University of Nottingham has studied the phenomenon of slavery for decades, and he concludes that slavery is alive and well today. He estimates that there are around 35 million slaves currently, including some in Germany, the heart of Europe; some aid organisations estimate that there are around 100 million slaves worldwide. Apart from those, Bales reckons that there are another 600 million people around the world "vulnerable" to becoming slaves. The drivers of slavery are the lack of jobs, drought, climate change and malnutrition.

The main difference between slavery now and in the past is the price. Following an interview with Prof Bales, the German TV station *Deutsche Welle* reported: "Perhaps the only thing entirely *new* about modern slavery is the collapse of the price of slaves. Adjusted for inflation, the average price of a slave through the centuries has been about $40,000. The average price today: $100. The highest price for a slave is roughly $10,000, and in his research Bales encountered an example of debt bondage in India that was as cheap as 62 *cents*. Why the price collapse? It is largely due to the sudden increase of the global population. Since World War II, it has expanded from 2 billion people to over 7 billion today, which is entirely unprecedented. Unlike before, there is an endless supply of labour from large populations of people who are begging for work. The result of this price collapse is the hallmark of modern slavery: disposable people. Rather than purchasing a slave for life, modern slaveholders simply use people as slaves for short periods of time – until they can no longer be exploited – and then they are simply replaced by others."[18]

Yet, for some reason, we are always being told that if we just get more people in the world, things will be better. This year, Singapore's *Today Online* wrote: "[China's] shortages of workers, students and babies are set to worsen at an alarming rate."[19] In Singapore, we are often warned about a "demographic time bomb" as the population gradually ages.[20] Here, like in most countries, having children is encouraged and financially subsidised. In a "green" country like Denmark, mothers are given DKK18,024 (about $3,000) each year per baby, dropping to $1,870 per year when the child turns 7.[21] Fertility treatment is free.

In reality, population decline is not a time bomb; population growth is the time bomb. In the case of China, there are many indications that their one-child policy – only recently relaxed – could actually have paid off. The extreme poverty rate fell from 88% in 1981 to 12% in 2010. In India, where the population is similar in size but much younger and growing faster, the poverty rate fell much less, from 60% to 33%, over the same period.[22]

So China is doing the right thing by controlling its population. At the other extreme, when I was born in 1952 there were some 20 million people in the Philippines, and the country was in pretty good shape. Today there are 106 million, of whom 22 million live below the official poverty line – more than the total population used to be! Another 10 million have been forced to move abroad where they work as cheap labour. According to government statistics, there are some 4 million drug users and criminal suspects, but the prisons are hopelessly overcrowded. So since Rodrigo Duterte became president in 2016, it is alleged that some 12,000 suspects have been killed; there simply isn't room for them anywhere.[23] The state is basically taking superfluous people out of circulation in a systematic manner. If that is not an overpopulation crisis, I don't know what is.

So why are we constantly being encouraged to have more and more babies, when in fact overpopulation is destroying the earth and making us all worse off in the end?

One reason is our obsession with nominal GDP growth. Yes, on the surface of it, more people will produce a higher domestic product; that is obvious. But what is important is not the nominal GDP, but rather the GDP per capita, as well as our general quality of life, which should include a healthy environment and plenty of personal space for everyone. Space is valuable; a big house is more expensive than a smaller one. A business class ticket costs more than flying coach. When the bus is half full, the passengers don't cram next to each other at the back, they spread out on all the seats. Already many years ago, the British zoologist Desmond Morris wrote a brilliant book, *The Human Zoo* (1969), where he showed that people in crammed urban environments show symptoms similar to neurotic animals locked up in cages. So there is a premium to space; we don't know exactly what it is worth, but it has a price – a price that is paid when it disappears.

And then of course there is the old song: We have an ageing population; we need more young kids to take care of all the old people. This is simply not true. Let me take a minute or two to explain why, since this is important.

It is generally accepted in demographic studies that as a society matures and becomes more affluent, the Demographic Transition Model (DTM) kicks in. Briefly, this model states that societies go through five stages as they progress; from an early stage of excessively high birth rates and low life expectancy – such as most African countries today – to a mature stage (stage three and four) where the fertility rates come down below the 2.1 child-per-woman replacement rate and the population stabilises; gradually the population pyramid will lose its huge base of young people and become more keg-shaped and top-heavy. At stage five of the DTM, the society will progress into an ageing population with smaller families and a gradually declining population.

So the subject of population growth is different in various countries and at various levels of development, but the conclusion is always the same: Population growth stifles national development and makes us all poorer. Development economists have shown that population growth is detrimental to economic and social development in developing nations. In agricultural communities, the family farm gets carved into smaller and smaller lots as the family size increases, ultimately causing economic collapse, mass migration and possibly social conflict. In his book *Collapse* (2011), Jared Diamond devotes a whole chapter to describing the 1994 genocide in Rwanda and its many causes; overpopulation was definitely one of them.

In this day and age, mass migration out of Sub-Saharan Africa via a failed state like Libya into Europe has all the hallmarks of people escaping from overpopulation and associated environmental and social degradation. The migrants travel in chaotic fashion into a continent that is already packed full of people, with lots of small children in tow that they cannot afford to bring up. The current conflict in Syria is now widely accepted to have been caused

Human Population 1 AD to 2050 AD (projected)
(billions)

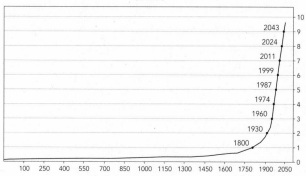

It is obvious that the human population explosion happened after the Industrial Revolution (around 1760), when fossil fuels, engines and mechanised agriculture allowed us to feed a larger number of people. The Demographic Transition Model posits that the population will level off and decrease with advanced development; but we urgently need to speed up that process.

33

by the population exceeding the carrying capacity of the land in a period of climate change-induced drought. That is how serious the overpopulation disaster can get.

Population control is rarely a popular topic; in fact it is often seen as taboo. How many kids you have is a very personal choice. But we need to recognise that overpopulation is not only an environmental problem, it is existential. And this recognition has to be translated into policy changes here and now; we urgently need to discourage further growth. In developing countries with persistently high birth rates, we need to leapfrog across the DTM stages quickly; we cannot wait for every person on Earth to get rich – we simply don't have the resources for that, so that is not going to happen. But empowering and educating women has been proven to speed up the DTM process.[24] Apart from that, a one-child policy is the best way forward for those societies.

Stage five countries include Japan and Russia; many others like Germany and Singapore are at stage five in reality but augment their populations through immigration. In affluent communities like those, we need to stop subsidising babies and fertility treatment, which in effect means taking resources from people who do the right thing and giving them to others. Regarding the elderly in those countries, most of those have plenty of resources to see them through. With better diet, exercise and healthcare they can work longer and have productive and fulfilling lives. The elderly will have savings and houses and stuff that the smaller younger generations can take over. In a way it is really quite logical, isn't it? If you have one child, he/she gets a bigger inheritance than if you have three or four or five, right?

Primatologist and conservationist Jane Goodall is a patron of Population Matters, a UK charity that addresses population size and the environment. She says in an interview: "It's our population growth that underlies just about every single one of the problems that we've inflicted on the planet".[25] With the understanding of global warming gaining traction, it is interesting to note that a new study published in *Environmental Research Letters* concludes that while living car-free will cut 2.4 tons of CO_2 emissions per year, having one child fewer will save 58.6 tons; it is by far the best decision you can make for the planet![26]

2

Too Much Is Not Enough

"Blessed are the young for they shall inherit the national debt."

— HERBERT HOOVER

The debt trap

In the previous chapter, I quoted Clive Ponting as saying that economic forces are behind our problems with habitat destruction, species extinctions and global warming. I completely agree. In fact, that was the main reason I retired as a naturalist, wildlife photographer and producer and marketer of nature books in 2013. At the time, I felt we had plenty of beautiful pictures and information about our natural world. By now we know pretty much what is out there, and we know what is going on. So if we want to conserve what we have left, it is not more studies of ecology that we need; it is more studies and understanding of the dynamics that cause our environment to deteriorate in the first place. These drivers are social in nature, and – as Ponting points out – in the final analysis they are rooted in economics and finance.

In fact, I would like to be even more specific and narrow this down further. In my view, *debt* is behind it all. Debt has many names – credit expansion, leverage, liability, financial obligation – but in the end it all means the same thing: You use money you don't have; you live beyond your means, hoping and dreaming that someday you will be able to pay it back. We treat the environment the same way; collectively, we take more out of the earth than we can ever replace. In reality, we are wrecking the earth on borrowed funds and borrowed time.

How did this debt trap come about? Let me give a brief explanation here. It started in the 1970s. At that time, the exceptional global economic expansion starting in 1948 was about to be exhausted. In the US, welfare entitlement payments from programmes established during the booming 1960s, as well as further expenditures from the Vietnam War, put strains on public finances and private investments. Capital started flowing out of the US into Europe; the gold standard established at the Bretton Woods meetings in 1944 could no longer be honoured, and then President Nixon declared in August 1971 that the dollar could no longer be exchanged for gold at a fixed price of $35 per ounce. From then on, in effect, the US could expand their money supply and their debt indefinitely. The final trigger came during the first oil crisis in 1973. Oil went from $3 to $12 per barrel, and in 1979 it tripled to $36. In other words, the price of the fossil fuels that had been essential for our industrialisation went through the roof.

Rather than accept that the earth was telling us to slow down, we ignored the warning signs. Instead of adjusting our production and consumption and reducing our global footprint on the environment, we accelerated our expansion. How? By borrowing! In the world's largest economy, the electorate chose the amiable but poorly trained Ronald Reagan to run the country. During the election campaign in 1980, his opponent, incumbent Jimmy Carter, ran on a platform of austerity; he didn't stand a chance. Reagan promised voters what they wanted: more money at all cost. With that began a spiral of public and private debt – as well as the trade deficits – which allowed Americans to maintain the lifestyle they had gotten accustomed to during the 1950s and 60s, a period which had seen real welfare improve through higher productivity.

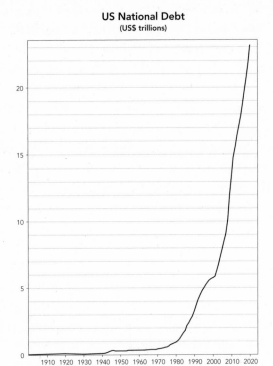

US National Debt
(US$ trillions)

This chart shows US government debt projected till 2020.

The perception of growth was achieved through continuous expansion of the money supply (M2); except the new money wasn't being distributed equally throughout the economy. Wages stagnated with the erosion of the American productive base, while profits – return on capital – went up, and prices of assets such as shares and houses increased. Those who had plenty of those – assets – got richer and richer. Those who only had their wages to rely on went nowhere.

Please note that the chart above only shows sovereign American debt (currently around $19 trillion); it is held mainly by domestic agencies such as social security funds, the Federal Reserve and some private mutual funds. Some 32.5% of that debt is owned by foreign investors, mainly China, Japan, UK, Brazil and others.[27] But on top of that comes private mortgage-backed debt (at around $8 trillion), as well as corporate and consumer debt. Some debt hawks sometimes also add future contracted liabilities to the debt, the so-called future entitlement spending, and they then come up with astronomical figures in the $80 trillion region, but we will leave that aside here.

Either way you slice it, the "deficits don't matter" debt model was followed by all the major economies and still is today. Here is a chart showing gross government debt, not in nominal terms but as a percentage of the yearly output of the economy as measured by the GDP:

Gross Government Debt
(as % of GDP)

Japan takes a clear lead, but all major economies are really in on it.

While the debt has expanded, savings rates have declined. In the US, personal household savings rates as a percentage of GDP have declined from 10–12% during the 1960s, 70s and even into the 80s to single digits after that. In 2017 the savings rate was a miserable 2.4%. It is somewhat higher in Europe and even higher in East Asia and especially Japan, but look at the situation in Africa:

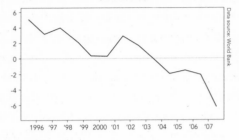

Adjusted Net Savings in Sub-Saharan Africa
(as % of GNI)

Data source: World Bank

In Sub-Saharan Africa, personal savings rates have dropped into negative territory; this continent is in real trouble.

The end of history?

So this is the script that most modern economies have followed ever since the 1970s: They borrow and borrow and then borrow some more. After the collapse of the Soviet Union in 1991 and the unravelling of the whole socialist sphere – the Second World that no longer exists – the consensus was that a planned economy didn't work. So everyone agreed that a new unified world order – a mixed market economy built on credit expansion and mass production of consumer goods – would be the future. Liberal democracies would in perpetuity give the electorate what they had always wanted: more money forever.

Let me quickly give one consideration to the debate: Can dictatorships produce as much prosperity as democracies? Do people even care? This is a complex issue that is really out of the scope of this book, but for what it is worth, it is my personal observation that over time economics overrides everything else, including type of government. Dictatorships tend to fall only when they can no longer produce the goods, when people starve. As long as they facilitate economic prosperity and plenty of consumer goods they are tolerated, China being our current prime example of that. And then we will go on.

1992 was also the year that Bill Clinton was voted into office as the 42nd President of the US. And yes, for a while it really looked like this could be the end of history. A short period of economic upswing started, the American national debt even levelled out for a brief period of time. This was driven by the increasing use of electronic data processing and the improved productivity associated with that. Remember, even Bill Gates didn't need a secretary anymore. On top of that came a huge expansion of the global labour force, as people in the formerly communist states of Eastern Europe got a chance to participate in the global market economy; many of those countries joined the newly formed WTO and the EU. That kept wages down but production up. In China, some 250 million people moved out from the countryside during the 1990s to do higher-productivity work in factories and the cities.

But in our triumphant celebration of the final victory over oppression and poverty forever, we forgot to consider the limits to growth as usual. The new prosperity was built on a mountain of financial and ecological debt. Financially, the dot-com crash in 2000 brought the tech-heavy NASDAQ index down from 5,048 in March that year to 1,114 in October 2002. This event reminded us that trees don't grow to the sky. And ecologically, during the same period, the realisation started to set in that there might be a breaking point somewhere within the environment; we covered that in the first chapter.

History wasn't over after all. The 2000s brought with it new historic developments, not least the war on terror and a lot of other new wars and conflicts that we financed the way we always do – by issuing debt. Until the financial system finally reached its breaking point in September 2008. I was on a visit to Alaska with my family that month. The crisis played out day by day like a crime novel; no fiction writer could have produced a more gripping script. After we got back, Lehman Brothers filed for bankruptcy on 15 September – it was the largest bankruptcy in US history – and after that all hell broke loose.

THE ETHICAL INVESTOR'S HANDBOOK

True to form, the world's financial leaders refused to see the 2008–2009 financial crisis and subsequent Great Recession for what it was: a manifestation of excess; too much debt; a supply chain running on derivatives and leveraged instruments that was ravaging the earth. Here is how China reacted to the debt crisis – by issuing more of the same:

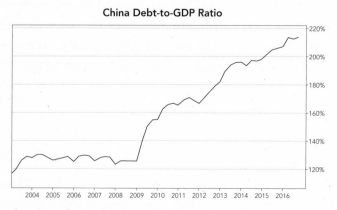

China Debt-to-GDP Ratio

This chart shows China's total debt-to-GDP ratio. It is now over 200% and growing!

In the US, Europe and Japan, governments and central banks got busy manipulating the economy to kick the debt can further down the road. Their weapon of choice: monetary policy.

Monetary weapons of mass (environmental) destruction

Did you know that in 1981 the average US mortgage rate on a 30-year fixed-rate loan was 17%; and that it reached 18.5% in October that year?[28] I remember those days; it was a great time to be investing in fixed income (bonds)! But a whole generation of young people today did not live through that. They might think that interest rates have always been as low as they are now, and always will be. In 2018 that same rate was around 4%. Back in 1981, the interest on a US 10-year Treasury bond hovered between

12.6% and 14.6% per annum; by 2018 it was down to 2.8%, and even dropped as low as 1.4% a few years prior to that.

When the 2008 financial crisis hit and as markets bottomed out in March the following year, the knee-jerk reaction from governments and central banks was to bail out the large banks and insurance companies – which had been instrumental in generating the crisis in the first place! Instead of using this once-in-a-lifetime opportunity to clean out the oversized financial sector and slow down our extractive exploitation of the earth, we got more of the same. A programme initiated and co-ordinated by the central banks in all the major economies of buying up the debt and lowering interest rates penalised those who saved and rewarded those who lived beyond their means.

In her thought-provoking book, *Makers and Takers: How Wall Street Destroyed Main Street*, Rana Foroohar accounts for the events before and after the Great Recession in much more detail than I ever could. But since my mission here is to identify the link between our economy, finance and ecological disintegration, let me just talk about one issue: our interest rate policies.

In an opinion piece on the website Eco-Business in February 2017, I highlighted the occasion when then-chair of the US Federal Reserve (the American central bank), Janet Yellen, accepted that climate change could have (negative) consequences for the financial system. In her testimony before the US Senate Banking Committee, Yellen said: "We recognise that risk events with severe weather and climate changes could have effects on the financial system."

This was a step forward, but personally I think we could go one step further and acknowledge that the central bank policies of low interest rates are in fact one of the very causes of environmental damage. Allow me to explain in some more detail, since this is important but not very well understood by mainstream economists. This is an extract of what I wrote in 2017:

We know that the environment has for decades provided limits to how much the aggregate economy can grow. We know that our way of calculating GDP is flawed. We count the depletion of natural capital as income, and we see the "uneconomic" growth of crime, accidents, wars, population growth and pollution as GDP increases, when in fact there is no improvement in social welfare from this type of expansion.

The recent financial crisis of 2008–2009 was the earth crying out that it has had enough, but we didn't listen. With easy monetary policies we allowed consumers to consume and companies to expand beyond what market forces and prudent financial policies would allow. We have too much steel in China; too much oil in the US.

Much of this extractive production ends up in storage facilities or is dumped on the market at low prices; eventually it ends up dumped all together in landfills and as atmospheric pollution.

This mechanism works because of quantitative easing and the Federal Reserve's large-scale asset purchases, which has pushed up the price of junk bonds from mining and fracking companies to inflated levels. The financial expansion and the environmental damage, including climate change consequences, go hand in hand. We are basically wrecking the earth on borrowed funds and borrowed time.

Now that an environmental issue – climate change – has grabbed the attention of the mainstream economic academic community for the first time ever, this acceptance has to be translated into policy.

To reduce environmental damage and associated climate change, we need a monetary policy that supports prudent financial management. We need to get back to the old concept from pre-1980s economics where capital was deferred spending, not an ever-expanding supply of cheap electronic money.

We all have a role to play in reducing the risk of environmental collapse. Individuals can control their spending and use their powers as political consumers; companies can respond to those new consumer habits and allocate investments accordingly.

Since they now officially accept the risk, central banks – like the one Janet Yellen is in charge of – can raise interest rates quickly to cool down the extractive and capital-heavy parts of the economy, reduce the broader money supply and ensure that banks and other financial institutions are well-financed to meet increased risk from inevitable insurance losses as well as so-called "stranded assets", i.e. carbon-intensive projects that are being made redundant by disruptions from the new carbon-light future economy.

Three immediate sets of policies from the Fed would facilitate this and be welcome from a climate change point of view:

1. Revert back to the so-called Taylor Rule for setting interest rates. Very simply, this would target interest rates to be the inflation rate plus 2%.

2. Reduce the Fed's balance sheet by not re-investing its holding of treasuries and mortgage-backed securities at maturity. This would contract the money supply and reduce the price of other bonds, including corporate bonds from polluting industries.

3. Raise the reserve as well as the capital
    requirements for commercial banks to avoid
    excessive risk-taking and discourage the debt
    culture that is harming the environment.
    Ideally banks should only lend out money they
    have, and not use financial gearing at all.[29]

Interesting rates

I stand by all that today. As I write, the ECB (European Central
Bank) deposit rate is -0.4% p.a. Yes, you read it correctly: negative 0.4%! A historical and economical abomination that is causing
huge distortions in the European economy where young people
cannot afford to buy a decent home – as the low rates push up
asset prices – while pensioners suffer, because pension funds
cannot generate a decent return on their portfolio of fixed income
securities.[30]

I take my son (born 2002) to the bank once in a while and
help him deposit his *hongbao* money that he gets from family and
friends during Chinese New Year. But it is really a pointless exercise. I wish I could tell him that you get rewarded in this world
if you save – like I did when I was his age – but I cannot. In our
economy, capital has no value and you are stupid if you save it; you
simply lose out. A DBS Autosave account in SGD pays no interest,
but it charges a S$2 monthly service fee, S$7.50 if your average
balance falls below S$3,000.[31] You would be better off if you closed
the account and simply kept your cash at home under the mat-
tress. Yes, inflation at around 2% p.a. would slowly eat it up, but
at least you wouldn't have to pay the bank on top of that.

It doesn't have to be like that. What has happened is that decades of financial engineering – the general financialisation of the
economy that Foroohar explains so well – has transferred value
from the real economy (Main Street) into the financial sector
(Wall Street). In the specific case of Singapore, where finance and

insurance services account for some 13% of the economy, many people work in that sector and have benefited from this.[32] But in general, the public simply has more bankers, fund managers, financial advisers and insurance agents to feed, i.e. more fees to pay and this way less money for themselves. The notional amount of outstanding contracts in the interest rate derivatives market – the largest such market in the world – was some $542 trillion in July 2017.[33] But in the meantime, my son cannot get any interest on his savings!

In economics, the Taylor Rule teaches that nominal interest rates should usually be higher than the prevailing inflation rate, i.e. the loss in value of fiat money over time. It really seems intuitively quite logical, doesn't it? During periods of high inflation and high economic output, the nominal rate should be increased; vice versa during periods of recession and low inflation.

Mathematically, the Taylor Rule goes like this:

$$i = r^* + pi + 0.5\,(pi - pi^*) + 0.5\,(y - y^*)$$

i is the nominal federal funds interest rate, r^* is the real rate (adjusted for inflation) and pi is inflation rate. In other words, r^* constitutes the so-called "neutral rate" which John Taylor – who developed the formula – pegged at 2%. The two other factors are inflation rate minus the target rate, plus the real output in the economy minus the potential output. You can play around with those if you have sufficiently accurate data, but you can also ignore those if the economy runs on track. So in essence, the formula says that nominal interest rates should be inflation rate plus 2%. Since the current inflation rate in the US is about 2.2%,[34] nominal interest rates should be approximately 4%; yet they are only 1.75% currently, and although rising slowly they are way too low to compensate savers and reduce wasteful activity in the economy.

A note to readers in Singapore, who may not be aware of this: In this country – which has an extremely open economy – a fairly unique monetary policy is in place. Here, interest rates are set by the banks, not by the Monetary Authority of Singapore (MAS), the central bank. Instead, MAS conducts monetary policy by tweaking the exchange rate of the Singapore dollar.

While monetary policies deal with interest rates and the money supply in the economy, fiscal policies deal with public taxation and expenditure. Central banks are in theory financial institutions independent of governments, although in reality economic policies are somewhat co-ordinated by various public institutions. Taxation and expenditure (i.e. subsidy) policies have a direct impact on investors and your capital allocation choices, but we will look at that a little later.

Monetary as well as fiscal policies have created a world economy with many imbalances and contradictions, all in all a difficult situation to navigate for investors. We have both too little and too much. Let me try to explain this briefly.

Shortage or oversupply?

When my first book came out in 2016, I gave an interview on the financial internet channel FinanceAndLiberty.com. The editor gave it the dramatic title: "COLLAPSE is inevitable. Here's why." During the interview I explained how the trinity factors of limited resources, pollution and financial instability would limit our ability to grow the aggregate economy going forward, and on that basis I advised everyone to position themselves correctly for an uncertain future, to be a "financial doomsday prepper", a term I also used in a guest blog for the Singapore financial website TheFinance.sg.[35]

After my American interview, a number of listeners wrote in. Some appreciated the points I made; some didn't. Comments ranged from "One of your most lucid guests" and "I agree on all points" to "There are tons of resources and climate change is a yet to be proven science". But let me dwell on this one: "Bullsh*t. If raw materials (like metals & petroleum) were 'scarce', their prices would be higher. But what do we have instead? Declining oil prices, declining base metal prices, stagnant precious & earth metals prices. He didn't provide any explanation of this disconnect."

Indeed, there does appear to a disconnect here, and maybe I didn't explain it fully on that occasion. So let me try now, for the benefit of that listener and others who might find this puzzling: We have both too much and too little of everything!

The world is a confined space, and you cannot expand forever in one of those. Studies such as the Living Planet Report 2016 – popularised by the WWF – show that we are consuming resources as if we had 1.6 Earths at our disposal.[36] We don't, we only have one, so ecologically we are running on the fumes. We are depleting virtually every natural resource you can think of. In *What Has Nature Ever Done For Us?* (2013), Tony Juniper puts it this way: "The approach taken towards natural capital is rather like a planetary Ponzi scheme." Meaning, like crooks do, we pay dividends not with profits but by depleting our capital till it runs out.

It is all pretty obvious if you care to look into this, and I will not go into too many detail here, but let me highlight one less-often discussed resource: phosphorus. This element is essential for making mineral fertilisers, without which we could only produce about half the food we produce today. However, the supply of phosphorus is finite, and it cannot be recycled; with increased demand and limited supply, there have been warnings about an impending shortage crisis.[37]

Correct, as my listener friend said, then by right market forces should kick in. Theoretically, prices of scarce goods should rise and adjust demand downwards to meet supply. But that cannot happen if you put unlimited excesses of monetary liquidity out there in circulation. Or if you keep interest rates so low that cheap capital doesn't reflect the true cost of extracting the resources. Or if you have too many people desperate for work, who just want to dig and dig and dig for a few dollars a day.

Take the price of petroleum that my listener brought up; a product that I actually know a bit about having worked in the oil business for 10 years and also out of sheer interest in it. The artificially low interest rates in the US during this decade allowed oil companies to issue expensive bonds and raise lots of capital for their fracking (enhanced recovery) operations. Unemployed workers – excess labour anxious for stuff to do – gladly got involved with these problematic operations at low wages; all the cheap crude oil and natural gas on the market depressed prices. But that doesn't mean that scarcity is no longer an issue; it just means that the market forces have been put out of work. We are sucking hydrocarbons out of tight shale formations in the Permian Basin, out of the high Arctic and up from deep waters off Brazil, where it is really better being left alone. Unless we develop viable alternative energy sources fast, petroleum prices are bound to skyrocket again in the future when the supply of even these hard-to-reach marginal supplies is exhausted.

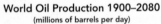

World Oil Production 1900–2080
(millions of barrels per day)

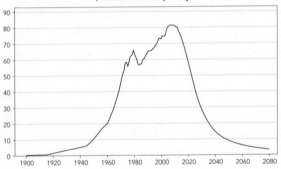

Right, we have a glut of oil at the moment, but according to the International Energy Agency, production is set to decline after 2020. What will this do to prices? The IEA says that more electric cars and alternative energy sources "is enough to keep prices within a $50–70/barrel range to 2040".[38] Really? Personally I am not so sure about that, but we will see!

Like I stated before, we are wrecking the earth on borrowed funds. So if we really want to help the planet, we should campaign for an end to QE, higher interest rates and a shrinking population!

The fact is that virtually every mineral and element and resource you can think of on Earth is diminishing. Artificially manipulated commodity prices cannot conceal that reality. Heck, we are even running low on sand! Who would have imagined that a few decades back? Developers, construction companies and land reclamation contractors in Singapore are on a constant search for new sources of sand. Indonesia and Vietnam closed their markets a few years back; people in Cambodia are not too happy about their river deltas being dredged out; Malaysia is reviewing the sand trade on a case-by-case basis.[39] There is always Myanmar, of course – they are still selling us their stuff, but for how long? The problem is not restricted to Singapore. All over the Asia-Pacific region and even in parts of Africa, Europe and North America, the shortage of sand and the environmental costs of excessive extraction have become economic and ecological issues.

So what do we have too much of? Manufactured stuff, as well as all the by-products and garbage that go with it. We also have too much capital and too much labour and too many people in general for the earth to cope. Anything that we people can make, we have too much of. Where is the shortage? In natural capital: good land, healthy forests, clean water and fresh air. We will deal with that in more detail in the next chapter. But before we move on from the economics of this, let us consider an important question regarding the enormous liabilities we have accumulated.

What will happen to the debt?

Yes, that is the trillion-dollar question. What will happen when all this debt has to be unwound? How can the American government suddenly pay $19 trillion back to lenders? They cannot now, of course, and they probably never will. In fact, each year – as we saw above – governments add to the debt; voters demand it. If the current government doesn't do it, the constituents will find new politicians who will. Each time, we are being told that there is nothing to worry about, because future growth will settle the debt.

Here is what Paul Mason says about that statement in his book *Postcapitalism*: "Unless the future delivers spectacular riches, none of this [debt] is sustainable. But the kind of economy that's emerging from the crisis cannot produce such wealth." I agree, and I would add: The resources are not there; and if we try to spur on such growth the conventional extractive way, pollution will kill us.

So something else will have to give. In the case of the US, it could be a serious decline of its currency. It could also be a re-emergence of inflation, or it could be a world-wide recession and banking crisis. In 2013 we had such a crisis in the small country of Cyprus in the Mediterranean. It was solved by so-called bail-ins (not bail-outs); in other words, depositors' money was confiscated and used to salvage the banking system. We could see something like that on a larger scale in other, more important, insolvent countries.

All this might not happen for a while, so don't run out and sell all your stocks and bonds tomorrow and buy gold and silver and platinum and hide it in a bunker in the woods. As we have seen, governments and central banks have played the debt game for decades, almost as long as I have been around. They are pretty good at it by now, so it seems likely that they can play it for a while longer. Then-chair of the Federal Reserve Janet Yellen said during an interview in 2017, while the Fed was raising the federal funds rate a few times yearly in 0.25% increments, that they were doing this... so that they could lower them again later! In other words, the accommodative monetary policy will only stop when it hits a brick wall, and when that will happen is anyone's guess.

And don't rely too much on guidance from the mainstream investment advisers parading on financial television every night in fancy suits. Remember the November 2016 American presidential election? The market consensus at the time was that a Donald Trump victory would result in a 13% stock market correction. Yes, the markets went down for a day or two, then they started reversing. The S&P 500 index ended up going from 2,191 in November 2016 to 2,872 in January 2018, a 30% increase! So much for professional advice.

As an investor, you are pretty much on your own. So that is why I urge you to be aware of the risks out there in the system. Too many "expert" presenters have a hidden agenda in their message, even if they are not upfront about it or even quite unaware of it themselves. Personally I take every statement or opinion with a grain of salt if it comes from someone who works for the government, a university or a corporation or who is running for election. One of the few hedge fund managers that I admire, Jeremy Grantham, says in one of his interviews that in the financial sector, telling it like it is amounts to an invitation to get fired. Who does that leave? Pundits, who just invest their own money – listen to them!

In general, try not to contribute to the problems I have highlighted here. Do the right thing and stay solvent and prepared. Then, if and when another crisis hits, you will be ready and positioned to ride it out, maybe even benefit from it. I will give you some tips on how you can do that a little later in the book. But first of all, it is important that we preserve, protect and grow all the capital we have, financial as well as natural.

3

Natural Capital

"You cannot eat money."
— ALANIS OBOMSAWIN

All we need is... more natural capital

In the previous chapter, we saw how central bank policies encourage economic expansion. But isn't that good, you might say; don't we need growth? People in politics – as well as financial experts – always cheer when stock markets accelerate, when GDP is up, when new mines and skyscrapers and factories and shopping malls open up. One Belt, One Road. Growth must be good, right? They all say it is.

I grew up reading Hans Christian Andersen stories. I loved them then, and it is a sign of the author's genius when you can read them 60 years later and still find them relevant. Try to read *The Little Match Girl* and tell me if you are not touched, or *The Nightingale* or *The Ugly Duckling*. But my favourite is *The Emperor's New Clothes*. Crooked tailors pretend to weave expensive new garments for the Emperor out of nothing; both he and his ministers are too insecure and afraid to be called stupid to object. It takes an innocent little boy in the crowd to finally call out that the Emperor is actually parading around naked. Personally I think we should consider the possibility that no matter what everyone says, our economic values and priorities are in reality equally flawed.

When we all repeat this mantra to each other – that economic growth is good – we tend to overlook the issue of natural capital. Natural capital is the earth's stock of soil, water, air, forests and other natural resources, assets that are essential for all life on the planet, including our own. In his book *Natural Capital: Valuing the Planet* (2015), Dieter Helm argues for a concept he calls the "aggregate natural capital rule". In a nutshell, the rule states that we should preserve our total stock of natural capital in each country and on the planet as a whole. Dr Helm strongly believes that to avoid an environmental collapse, we should replace the non-renewable natural resources we use in the course of our development – such as minerals and fossil fuels – with renewable natural resources and habitat restoration projects, for example the planting of new forests, restitution of wetlands, and so on, thereby leaving the total "balance sheet" of natural capital unchanged or better. For the benefit of future generations, "the aggregate level of natural capital should not decline", he writes.

Dr Helm is painfully aware that at the moment we are not doing enough of this. In the first chapter I covered some of the horror stories of unsustainable development; they are all around us and plain to see for anyone who cares to look. In fact, many of the natural resources that we used to consider renewables are increasingly being shifted into the non-renewable category, like oceanic fish stocks, primary tropical rainforests and even farmland, which are being exploited beyond their threshold of recovery. Nevertheless, Dr Helm maintains a positive outlook: "There is no reason why our environmental problems cannot be tackled... It is perfectly possible to achieve sustainable economic growth." We have the financial resources to replace the non-renewable natural capital we destroy, and Dr Helm identifies economic policies to facilitate this transfer: compensation, environmental taxes and subsidies, and permit payments.

Conserve your personal capital

Others might disagree with this – that economic growth is sustainable – but Dr Helm believes it can be done. He points repeatedly throughout his book to one particular role model of his: the Norwegian government. The Norwegians are doing exactly what he wants the whole world to do. They are exploiting a non-renewable resource – the offshore North Sea oil and gas fields – but instead of squandering it, they accumulate the financial capital generated, most of it in the so-called Government Pension Fund Global. In 2017, the value of the fund exceeded US$1 trillion, making it the largest sovereign wealth fund in the world.

Other state participants in the North Sea oil and gas bonanza – the UK, Denmark and the Netherlands – did not accumulate the windfall generated from tax revenues; they simply spent it. In extreme cases such as Venezuela and Nigeria, natural capital extraction turned into a national curse, not a cure.

So what can we learn from these events? The moral is that with honest, efficient and prudent public governance, we can accomplish a lot. Today the Norwegians are hailed internationally as macroeconomic management shining stars, and also as environmental pioneers, conserving financial capital and spending a lot of it at home and abroad on natural capital restoration. In 2010 the Norwegian government donated US$1 billion to the REDD programme in Indonesia, for instance – with limited results, admittedly, but at least they tried.[40] We will come back to REDD in Chapter 10.

But there is another lesson in all this for me. As individuals it is difficult for each one of us to influence public policies and macroeconomic events. But we can always strive to get our own house in order; on a personal level we can do what Dr Helm advises on a national scale. We will be better off if we conserve our own personal capital and direct it into a sustainable path of consumption and investment.

As I covered in the first two chapters of this book, the environmental problems facing us are gigantic and unprecedented but also by now well documented. Furthermore, we are growing the economy on an exceptional expansion of financial debt. At US$217 trillion, the current global debt is more than three times the global GDP[41]; we are in uncharted waters, and we simply don't know what will happen when this bubble bursts. So for each one of us as individuals, now is not the time to get into more debt. In fact, try to build up financial muscle, just like successful countries such as Norway and Singapore do, but on a personal level.

I started work on the Norwegian offshore oil rigs in 1974, when the industry was in its infancy; I later transferred to the UK and after that to Southeast Asia. I was never director or CEO of a large corporation; I never made a boatload of cash. But I did save the money I made, invested it carefully and retired from the oil business in 1986 when I was 33 years old. I never worked in engineering again. In fact, I have tried to do my bit for a better environment ever since. Anyone can do the same, if you put your mind to it and find out how. The secret is to control your spending while you work in a conventional job; you will not only help yourself, but also the planet. As we have seen, it is largely private consumption and associated waste that is choking the planet. So construct your own little "sovereign wealth fund" of quality assets to preserve your own capital – as well as the world's natural capital – and to ride out the uncertain times ahead. In the later chapters I will show you how to do that.

What is nature worth?

But before we get into that, let us consider what natural capital is worth. To be of value, nature must have a price, correct? Right, economists and ecologists have all tried to put a monetary value on nature and the ecosystem for decades. There is a whole field of economics – environmental economics – dealing with this, as well as a related field, ecological economics, developed in the 1980s. Both schools of thought attempt to value ecosystems and account for the so-called negative externalities of conventional development models. The former is more rooted in conventional economics from an environmental point of view, while the latter puts stronger emphasis on ecology as a closed loop with an essential need for sustainability. For those who want to know more, there are plenty of textbooks and courses available from reputable educational institutions.

But this is usually where the road ends, at the educational institutions. My observation is that environmental concerns have a hard time transiting from the ivy towers of academia into the mainstream public domain. Yes, the various gloomy reports about ecological decline and biodiversity loss sometimes get a little coverage in the *Guardian* newspaper in the UK and other somewhat left-leaning media. But you rarely see these issues covered on Fox News, which people around the world actually watch. And more importantly, the surveys do not seem to translate into action or official economic and social policies. The destruction of our natural world continues unabated.

Consider this 2014 survey by Robert Costanza, which is often referred to in the media and environmental course material. Dr Costanza and his team set out to calculate the monetary value of 17 important ecosystems around the world, such as the marine biome, coral reefs, estuaries, rivers, lakes, terrestrial grasslands, forests, etc. They found that these ecosystems in total provided services worth $142.7 trillion that year; that was around double the global GDP in 2014. However, had it not been for deforestation, pollution and the loss of coral reefs and other vital habitats, the number would have been $165.8 trillion (using a previous study by the same team in 1997 as a benchmark). In other words, we lose ecosystems and services worth over a trillion dollars every year.[42]

An equally amazing study was spearheaded by Sir Robert Watson and came out in March 2018. Watson, who is chair of IPBES (the Intergovernmental Science-Policy Platform on Biodiversity and Ecosystem Services), makes a strong case that loss of biodiversity from habitat degradation, invasive species and chemical pollution is as much of a threat to humanity as climate change: "The best available evidence, gathered by the world's leading experts, points us now to a single conclusion: we must act to halt and reverse the unsustainable use of nature – or risk not only the future we want, but even the lives we currently lead."[43]

Is all this interesting? Both yes and no. The meticulous studies by these scientist are indeed somewhat interesting – to me, anyway, and others spellbound by our natural world and ecological foundation. But with regard to practical consequences, maybe not so much. Valuing nature is just theory, and will most likely remain just theory in the foreseeable future. Yes, I am aware of the PES – Payments for Ecosystem Services – pioneered by some countries, and those are all well and good; in 2018 it was reported that some 550 PES projects worldwide now account for some $36 billion in transactions.[44]

It sounds great, right? But that amount is what Apple Inc turns over in a couple of months, with no help from governments. Basically it seems to me that most people I know are more concerned about the price of the new iPhone than the fictive price of all the coral reefs in the world put together. The influential Canadian-American economist John Galbraith once said: "Economics is extremely useful as a form of employment for economists." Let me paraphrase that and say: "Ecology is extremely useful as a form of employment for ecologists."

A slightly different approach to our environmental issues has been attempted by Richard Sandor, chairman and CEO of Environmental Financial Products LLC. What Herman Daly is to ecological economics, Dr Sandor is to environmental finance.

Sandor has tried to develop financial instruments and policies to deal with the question of negative environmental externalities for decades; he is the first author of the excellent study "Environmental Markets: A New Asset Class" published in 2014 by the CFA Institute Research Foundation. In this study, he and his co-authors present a complete account of the reasons behind environmental market failures, and they propose concepts and mechanisms for dealing with them. Try to get a copy of the report; it is available online from the CFA Institute. If you find it a bit technical, just skip to Chapter 9: Conclusion: You Can Put a Price on Nature, and also check out Chapter 8: Sustainability and Associated Asset Classes, which has some specific advice for SRI investors.

Briefly, in this study and throughout much of his work, Dr Sandor suggests three solutions for mitigating negative externalities such as the rapid depletion of common resources and associated pollution: (1) command-and-control, (2) subsidies and/or taxes, and finally his preferred instrument, (3) cap-and-trade. All these are top-down state-run schemes combining heavy-handed national and super-national legislation with some market forces and derivatives trading, which is Dr Sandor's main expertise. All this is great, and personally I wish Dr Sandor and his distinguished academic associates all the best with their important work. But in the meantime, in the real world, the earth is crashing.

Do we care?

Personally I agree with Robert Watson that biodiversity conservation is no longer just a matter of conserving some animal species that few people have heard of and even fewer people care about. But I can also see that on the face of it, biodiversity doesn't really matter.

My wife has spent years campaigning for the conservation of hornbills, a group of large tropical rainforest birds. The Helmeted

Hornbill (*Rhinoplax vigil*) is critically endangered and facing global extinction, but how many people have actually seen one? I have, and it would be a huge loss to me, my wife and a few other people should it disappear from the face of the earth. But let's face it, for most people life would go on as normal; they don't really need the Helmeted Hornbill. Or any of the other wild animals, for that matter.

My teenage son and I were in Kinokuniya not too long ago, the largest bookstore in Singapore, an amazing business that has so far survived the onslaught of online shopping. From there we travelled to the library at the Esplanade – some 3 km away – and we didn't have to go outside once! You take the underground train a couple of stops and then walk through a maze of underground tunnels, till finally you take the elevator to your destination. There is a whole city being built underneath Singapore itself. People who work here drive from their condo basement car park to another underground car park; they never have to step outside. And they love it. Who needs a Helmeted Hornbill?

In Singapore, last time I checked, the Nature Society Singapore (NSS) had some 1,500 members; on Facebook they have about 12,300 "likes". This is how many people – in a nation with over 5 million – are concerned enough to pay a S$40 annual membership fee to support nature conservation. In this country the population is growing, but membership in NSS is declining year after year. And then consider this: At the same time, the Liverpool FC Supporters Club (Singapore) has 6,196 members and 16,5000 Facebook "likes". That is one football club in a country far from Singapore, yet more people find this interesting and important to be engaged in than the natural heritage and biodiversity of their surroundings.

For one, J.B. MacKinnon seems to agree with me on this. In *The Once and Future World* (2013) he explores various reasons for why we should protect nature, and he considers a number of different approaches – scientific, spiritual, activist – but he finally concludes: "In every case those who put the living planet as a whole ahead of short-term human interests remain a small minority."

The utilitarian reasoning for conserving nature has certainly failed. So nature is worth $142.7 trillion per year? Who cares? This makes no sense to the oil palm grower in Sumatra who cannot feed his seven children unless he cuts more forest and burns it. Or to the Nigerian who lives in a country with 178.5 million people – more than half of whom are below 19 – and a fertility rate per woman of 5.4; he has to go out into the woods and catch a monkey or a rat – so-called bushmeat – if he wants something to eat.[45]

At the moment, we really only need 103 species on Earth. These are the plants that give us 90 percent of our food. At some point, yes, biodiversity conservation might become imperative. But by then it will be too late. And we can live for a long time before that happens. MacKinnon (2013) says: "If you're waiting for an ecological crisis to persuade human beings to change their troubled relationship with nature, you could be waiting a long, long time."

I agree with MacKinnon when he says: "We can simply *prefer* a wilder world." But at the moment too few people prefer a wilder world, and that is why little is likely to change. So there are 1,500 card-carrying nature lovers in Singapore. In Denmark, the Society for Nature Conservation has 130,000 members. In Norway, the Green Party got 3.2% of the parliamentary vote in 2017; the same year in Germany, Die Grünen (The Greens) got a bit more, 8.9% of the vote. During the 2016 US presidential elections, Jill Stein with the Green Party got 1.4 million votes (about 1%). That is in general the level of support for green causes around the place.

Crooked accounting

Nature has a lot of benefits for us. Singapore's National Parks Board put out a promotional video in 2018 in which they highlighted five benefits of tropical forests. These forests (1) support biodiversity; (2) purify soil and – in the case of mangrove forests – protect coastlines; (3) clean the air of particles and CO_2; (4) cool the air and collect and store rain; and (5) provide recreational benefits.

In *What Has Nature Ever Done for Us* (2013), Tony Juniper covers these benefits of nature plus many more: The health benefits of cycling and jogging in nature, both physically and mentally; the pest-control services that wild birds provide; the pollinating services of insects; the pharmaceutical value of genetic material; all the usual utilitarian arguments. They are all so true and significant.

But I analyse finance, I look at monetary issues. In those terms, what is nature *really* worth? Not much. MacKinnon could only come up with two ways of monetising the ecosystem in a sustainable manner, without extracting stuff from it and wrecking it in the process: water conservation and eco-tourism. Did I miss anything? I don't think so! Currently, these appear to be the only services that the public will actually dig into their pockets voluntarily and pay for – to get clean water from a forested area, and to stay in a nice lodge and watch wildlife all day. That doesn't mean you cannot profit from nature conservation in other ways. It just means that most other ways – like carbon trading, biodiversity research, clean energy, etc. – require an element of state manipulation to work.

In all fairness to Juniper, his chapter "False Economy" considers the role of finance in environmental damage and he states: "Natural capital is the bedrock that underpins industrial, manufactured, social and financial capital... The decline in natural capital will be causing inevitable feedbacks that will impact on financial capital." So therefore: "The reason for sustaining natural capital is about *keeping the economy going*, not nature." The utilitarian argument again. I tend to agree. I personally believe that our erosion of natural capital, which appears to continue on autopilot, will have detrimental consequences on our standard of living and general welfare. In fact I believe that this process has already started, but has yet to be recognised by the majority of people.

The lack of recognition has a lot to do with the way we organise our macroeconomic accounts. We have a P&L account (profit and loss), but we don't have a national balance sheet. Like I said, one of my hobbies is looking at annual reports from various companies and seeing how they perform. Imagine a public company putting out their annual accounts with only the revenue listed. No cost of sales, no asset depreciation and no inventory of current assets and liabilities. The auditors would throw that piece of garbage out right away, the shareholders would revolt, and the company would be delisted from the stock exchange.

Yet, this is what countries do all the time. Indonesia counts only the money it makes from cutting the forest, sucking out crude oil and cleaning the fish out of the oceans. So the GDP grows, and the country appears to get richer, when in fact it is getting poorer and poorer as the national assets – the natural capital – are run down.

Then consider the issue of exponential growth. If a liquid in a bottle doubles every day and the bottle fills up after 30 days, when is the bottle half-full? After 29 days, right? On the last day it suddenly reaches it limits. The oceans around Indonesia are just like that – they are rapidly being emptied of fish and filling up with plastic instead, thereby reaching the limits of what is tolerable very fast.

Running in circles

The quote at the top of this chapter is from a much-repeated statement credited to Native American Indians of the Cree tribe and popularised by Alanis Obomsawin: "When the last tree is cut down, the last fish eaten, and the last stream poisoned, you will realise that you cannot eat money."[46] In a way this declaration reflects quite well on the issue of natural capital converted to financial capital.

We can accomplish a lot by manipulating financial capital; many people have gotten rich simply by shifting cash around. But financialisation also has its limits; as we have seen, central banks cannot solve all our problems simply by expanding QE, by printing more money. You cannot make everyone in a country a millionaire simply by giving each one a million dollars. Well, you can, but something else will have to give. Try putting a $100 bill on the table and see if it has grown after a year. Most likely it hasn't. Why not? Because you cannot generate value and wealth and prosperity from financial assets alone. Two important additional ingredients are required: work (including productivity), and in the case of manufacturing, material input.

So to protect our limited supply of natural capital and still preserve overall prosperity, it is imperative that we shift our economy into a different mode, one that requires less input of new materials. This mode has already been identified; it is called the circular economy.

Here is a diagram:

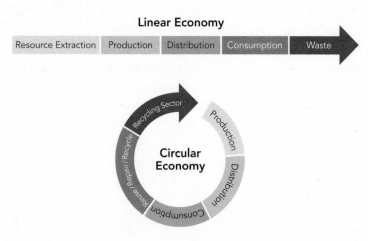

Notice that in the circular economy, waste disposal has been replaced with reuse and repair, while resource extraction has been replaced with recycling.

Recently a friend of mine came back from a trip to Raja Ampat, a snorkelling and diving site in the Indonesian province of West Papua, part of the famed Coral Triangle centre of marine bio-diversity. He said that in that area, mining companies are stripping off whole islands, simply bulldozing off all the topsoil to excavate nickel. Not only is this ruining the stunning tropical atolls, the exposed dirt runs into the ocean during downpours and covers the coral reefs. This is happening in spite of surveys that suggest that the ecosystem is worth more intact than the value of the minerals extracted, whether as fish spawning grounds or used sustainably for pearl cultivation or as eco-tourism destinations.[47] We simply have to step back and look at the drivers and mechanisms of coun-ter-production – i.e. uneconomic growth – of this magnitude.

So instead of continuously digging out new materials, the circular economy reuses what is already there. As an individual, you can do this right now simply by consuming less, by using your gadgets, clothes and other merchandise for longer and by buying pre-owned products – such as furniture – as much as possible. This is also cheaper, of course, and you can use the financial capital you accumulate this way to build up that private sovereign wealth of yours, which will see you through the hard times ahead. When you invest, source out opportunities to support participants in the circular – or shared – economy; this is where the future growth prospects are.

4

Winners and Losers

*"Winners never quit and
quitters never win."*

— TED TURNER

The Easter Island story

Before we leave the issue of natural capital versus man-made capital, allow me to briefly touch on the story of Easter Island. It has been used by many authors before me, but I feel it is important enough to reiterate. I think it holds some important lessons for our current planetary situation.

There are several slightly different versions of what happened to that remote community, but let me take my cue from Jared Diamond's *Collapse* (2011), since Diamond has visited the place and studied Easter Island as well as many other historical civilisations to find out why they failed.

Easter Island is one of the most remote and isolated places on Earth; it is a 164 sq km volcanic island in the South Pacific Ocean at 27° South, 109° West. The nearest populated place is Pitcairn Islands, more than 2,000 km to the west. Chile, to which Easter Island belongs today, is the nearest continental land, some 3,500 km to the east.

The Dutch explorer Jacob Roggeveen was the first European to visit the island; he landed on Easter Day 1722 and hence gave the island its name. He was puzzled to find an impoverished population of Polynesians with just a few patched-up and hardly sea-worthy straw canoes. The island had no trees, no animals and no other resources, yet hundreds of giant statues made of stone and on average over 6 metres high were everywhere along the coast. How could these statues have been built, moved and erected by the primitive people Roggeveen encountered? Two Spanish ships visited some years later in 1770, James Cook stopped by in 1774 and a British warship arrived in 1825. All were puzzled by the giant statues and the sorry state of the local population. By the time Cook arrived, the community had further deteriorated. Many of the statues were toppled over and the desperate population lived near starvation in caves dug into the barren hillsides with stone tools. They were in perpetual warfare with each other and were resorting to cannibalism; there was simply nothing else to eat on the island, other than people.

Only much later did researchers piece together a picture of what happened on Easter Island. The remote place was colonised by Polynesian people island-hopping from Southeast Asia eastwards across the Pacific. The last hop was pretty long and must have taken weeks, yet the early people managed to bring chickens and some crops like sweet potatoes with them in their catamarans. The first settlers, arriving around 600 AD, are believed to have numbered 20 to 30; they found an island pretty poor in resources, with few animals, no mammals at all, and the surrounding ocean not that rich in fish. However, the island had some 30 indigenous species of flora, including lush dense forests of palms and 15-metre-tall trees.

Over the following centuries the human population grew to over 7,000, possibly 15,000 at its peak around 1500. The people lived in settlements of wooden houses scattered across the island and organised in large family clans. Life was pretty good, and the settlers used their spare time to carve out and erect those giant stone statues that later puzzled the Europeans. In fact, the society of Easter Island was probably one of the most prosperous and well organised in the world at the time.

The society's downfall was deforestation. The forests were cleared and the natural capital converted into man-made capital such as houses and household items, canoes, fuel and poles to move the giant statues. With no large domesticated animals to help them, the people could only shift the 20-ton rocks across the island by rolling them on logs. All these efforts were a colossal waste of resources that the islanders could ill afford. The deforestation caused soil erosion; water sources dried up; there were no fertilisers on the island, so crops failed. Without trees, canoes could not be built and the fishing stopped; soon there were only a few chickens left to eat – and then people. Without proper boats there was no escape from the island.

We know that the economic collapse around 1600 was pretty sudden, because the residents abruptly abandoned a large number of unfinished statues at the rock quarry they had in the hills. The economic disintegration turned into social unrest and warring among the clans; stealing food and toppling each other's statues became perverse status symbols. By the time Roggeveen arrived, there were some 2,000–3,000 islanders left; it appeared that they had somehow managed to stabilise their miserable circumstances and eke out a meagre living from what little was left of the land. It was the arrival of Europeans that finally pushed them over the edge. The newcomers brought with them smallpox and other deadly diseases from which the islanders had no immunity. American and British slave ships started arriving and picked out the able adults. By 1877 there were only 110 old people and children left on the island; today, with help from the outside, the local community numbers some 6,000 people.

On a larger scale, Earth is like Easter Island. We have nowhere to run. We cannot all move to Mars or to another solar system – we don't have the technology or the resources. We are stuck here. If we destroy our entire habitat and spend our natural capital without conserving any, we will end up eating each other. The American media tycoon Ted Turner said so some years back during an interview: "We are too many people; that is why we have global warming... It will be 8 degrees hotter in 30 to 40 years, and basically none of the crops will grow, most of the people will have died and the rest of us will live like cannibals. The few people left will live in a failed state like Somalia or Sudan and living conditions will be intolerable."[48]

Personally I wonder what went through the guy's head when he cut down that last tree on Easter Island. Maybe he thought: "It's all about jobs!" Or: "We just need to get back to growth!" Or: "Deforestation is a hoax created by the Chinese; we must do more studies!"

Good governance is key

Right, the jury is still out on whether we will end up like Easter Island. But it is becoming increasingly apparent that we are in a world where conventional economic growth as we know it has reached its limits, where ecological constraints are closing in on us, constraints that could lead to serious environmental degradation and associated social unrest in the near future. So while the debate is on, you now need to consider: How do you navigate this situation that I have just described? From this chapter onwards, we will start to consider how you should position yourself as a participant in the economy and as an investor. Let us begin by looking at *where* you should be.

In *Be Financially Free*, I picked up an expression from one of my sources that I think will describe our future situation quite well: There will be islands of prosperity in an ocean of despair. I believe that this process has already started and that it will only be accentuated going forward. In this age of globalisation, individuals and families with a good education and some experience can move around the world fairly easily. So find your own winning formula, identify a place and a space that is ideal for you.

I got chatting with a foreign worker from Bangladesh here in Singapore last year; he asked me where I was from. He didn't quite know where Denmark was, but I explained that it was near Germany; he knew where Germany was. He asked me for advice. If he threw his papers away and travelled there – to Germany – would he be allowed to stay and work? He had heard that some people do that. I explained to him that it didn't work exactly that way, and I strongly advised him to stay in Singapore and make an honest living, hard as life here might be for semi-skilled labour. It would always be better than the humiliating life of an environmental refugee.

Bangladesh is one of those countries I would worry about, if I were the worrying kind. It is seriously overcrowded, and many people there are turning to Islamic fundamentalism and extremism for answers and solutions. It is one of the contributing sources to the 65 million people currently on the move away from overpopulation, ecological collapse and associated malnutrition, despair and social unrest. The number of displaced people in the world has never been higher.[49] A World Bank report in 2018 suggested that the number of what they call internal climate refuges could grow to 140 million by 2050, but obviously the actual number is anyone's guess.[50]

Clive Ponting quotes the IPCC as saying back in 2001: "Those with the least resources have the least capacity to adapt (to climate change) and are the most vulnerable." In my view, that would be correct for both individuals and countries. So make sure you have personal resources at your disposal, hold on to the money you make and grow it. And then try to find yourself a nice island of prosperity to be on.

I mentioned the plastic crisis plaguing Asia in the first chapter; but here is the good news: It doesn't have to be like that. When

I was a kid, my mother bought a small cottage on the west coast of Jutland in Denmark, facing the North Sea, as a recreational second home. The wide sandy beaches were grand, but covered in flotsam and plastic and glass bottles and discarded fishing nets. Today – some 40 years later – that beach is clean. What happened? People simply decided to do better.

When I worked on the oil rigs in the North Sea in those years, I was in the well service business, so I visited a lot of different rigs and platforms. When our crew first landed, we were usually given a briefing by the rig superintendent on safety and other procedures. We were always told that if you threw something over the side, you would be on the next chopper home. That included plastic coffee cups, gum wrappers, etc. – there was zero tolerance. Guess what? Nothing was thrown overboard! Authorities started tracking the ships between Great Britain and Denmark and cracked down hard on cases of illegal discharge of solid waste or liquids. Municipality workers combed the beaches on tractors and collected rubbish; the public took charge and stopped throwing it. There is very little garbage on the beaches facing the North Sea today.

Something similar happened to the Singapore River and the Kallang River when the Marina Barrage was built – a magnificent case study of ingenuity and foresight. I remember the 1980s when the Singapore River was tidal; at low tide the banks showed up with rats running out onto the mud to feed on the litter. Those waterways are cleaned up today, or almost cleaned up anyway; an environmental cleaner's job is never done! Contrast all this to a true story from Malaysia: A friend of mine was on a fishing trip off Mersing on the east coast, and he and his friends dutifully collected their garbage in dustbins on the boat during the excursion. As they were coming in to land at the harbour, the boat captain emptied the bins into the ocean!

Back in Singapore, Geh Min took her cue from natural – and not so natural – disasters around the world and wrote in 2018:

"We have seen how misguided thinking, based on insufficient knowledge and for short-term economic gains, has had long-term socio-economic costs, many of them almost impossible to reverse. Singapore should continue the legacy of thinking ahead on environmental issues and retain our competitive edge by more careful and informed environmental decisions." Dr Geh Min is a former nominated member of the Singapore parliament and former president of the Nature Society (Singapore). She concluded in her op-ed: "In fact, to prevent future disaster, we should be guarding our environmental reserves as carefully as we do our fiscal and social reserves."[51] Let me add: All countries should do just that!

In the previous chapter, we saw the stark contrast between how countries like Norway and Venezuela have handled their wealth of natural capital. Both are major oil and gas producers with additional large petroleum reserves. Yet, one country today stands out as a beacon of prosperity and prudent financial, environmental and social management. The other is a financial basket case and an international pariah; in 2016 Venezuela's economy contracted 19%, inflation was 800% and there was widespread unrest and chaos.[52]

What is the difference? If you had to sum it up in one word, it would be governance. If you had to use a few more, you could pick others such as democratic controls, strong public institutions, honesty, transparency, high levels of education, social cohesion, popular support for shared values and a supportive international network. Look for those factors when you select a place to work and live and retire. And, dare I say it, high national average IQ.

The "sensitive issue" of IQ

Something funny happened to me on 14 August 1983. I travelled a lot for work in those days, but I was home in Singapore to hear our prime minister at the time deliver his annual National Day Rally address live on television. This was an occasion that I would never miss; but on that particular day my jaw dropped when I heard Lee Kuan Yew bluntly say that the less-educated women in Singapore were having too many babies and the well-educated too few. The 1980 population census figures showed that tertiary-educated women had on average 1.6 children, while unschooled women had 4.4. The PM concluded that it was stupid (his words, not mine) for well-educated men to choose less-intelligent wives if they wanted their children to do well. Personally I had never heard a political leader be so direct and honest; I was flabbergasted. The speech led to a public uproar and, according to the PM himself, a 12% drop in votes for his party (the PAP) during the parliamentary elections the following year. Mr Lee paid a high price for being politically incorrect.

Later on, Mr Lee dedicated a whole chapter in his memoirs, *From Third World to First*, to this and related issues ("Nurturing and Attracting Talent").[53] The 1983 speech triggered what was then labelled the Great Marriage Debate in the press and among the public. Citing surveys and statistics, Mr Lee basically opined that nature accounts for 80% of a person's makeup, including IQ (Intelligence Quotient), and nurture only 20%. Some policy changes were implemented as a response to this, such as setting up the Social Development Unit to help better-educated men find suitable partners, and creating some incentives for graduate mothers to have more children. But by and large this was a "sensitive and divisive issue", in Mr Lee's own words; the matter was seen by many as hurtful to the poorly educated. Therefore the debate was gradually forgotten, and affirmative action for high-IQ individuals never became an important part of public policy, in Singapore or anywhere else.

But the issue of IQ will never go away. In his 2016 book *Hive Mind: How Your Nation's IQ Matters So Much More Than Your Own*, Garett Jones set out to show that the average IQ of a nation does matter. People who do well in the available tests obviously will do better in the educational system, but somewhat surprisingly numerous studies show that intelligent people also tend to share a number of other characteristics. High-IQ people are on average more patient, are able to wait longer for gratification, and tend to be more frugal financially and save more for the future. Smarter people are also generally better at cooperating, more generous, more reciprocating and more honest – and incidentally have quicker hand-eye coordination.

Jones's main point is that while it is no guarantee that you will automatically grow up to be happy just because you are smart, growing up in a high-IQ society will without doubt give you better opportunities in life, regardless of what your own IQ happens to be. High national savings rates, rule-based institutions, even the so-called Corruption Perception Index, all correlate positively with national average IQ. It might please some readers to know that Singapore, like much of East Asia, scores very high in both cognitive ability and IQ tests – 105 and 108 on average, respectively.

One striking chapter in Jones's book deals with the current average IQ in Sub-Saharan Africa. A survey in 2002 found that the national average IQ there was 67; after editing out data from certain impoverished areas, the researcher (Richard Lynn) raised this to 70. An opposing researcher (the much younger Jelte Wicherts) found this hard to accept and selected only the best test results, but still found that the average IQ for the continent was 76; that is at about the 5th percentile for a country like the UK (average 100). Wicherts concluded: "There can be little doubt that Africans average lower IQs than do Westerners."

So when you decide where to settle down – and considering the strong correlation between average national IQ levels and other indicators of quality of life – you would do yourself a favour if you cast political correctness aside for a moment and take a look at this table constructed by Richard Lynn showing average IQ test scores in selected countries.[54]

Rank	Country	Average IQ	Rank	Country	Average IQ
1	Hong Kong	108	12	Israel	95
1	Singapore	108	13	Vietnam	94
2	South Korea	106	15	Malaysia	92
3	Japan	105	16	Thailand	91
3	China	105	20	Indonesia	87
6	Switzerland	101	23	Iran	84
7	Norway	100	23	Nigeria	84
7	UK	100	23	Pakistan	84
8	Canada	99	23	Venezuela	84
8	Germany	99	25	India	82
8	Sweden	99	27	Kenya	80
9	Australia	98	30	South Africa	77
9	Denmark	98	34	Tanzania	72
9	USA	98	39	Haiti	67
10	Russia	97	43	Equatorial Guinea	59

However, keep in mind that there is more to national development than just IQ test scores. And perhaps most importantly, although we need to face the cold hard facts now and then, it is equally vital that we avoid antagonising, stigmatising and marginalising any groups whatsoever. We all need to work together, to get along and to find solutions going forward in a spirit of friendship, tolerance and cooperation.

When to be where

Like everywhere else in life, there are winners and losers when you look at the league of nations. Where you would want to settle is a very personal choice, and your preferences will most certainly change gradually over time. When you start out and have to build a career, the big cities of the world might be attractive – New York, Tokyo, London. This is where the jobs and the opportunities are, even though you might end up paying almost half your salary in rent, and a steep income tax on top of that! When you get married and have kids, you might like to move somewhere more family-oriented like Vienna, Melbourne, Vancouver, Auckland or, in Asia, Singapore. These places usually score among the highest in "liveable cities" surveys.

Then finally, when you become salary-independent and financially free, you will look for a good place to retire. Somewhere nice with a decent standard of living, low taxes and generally low cost of living to stretch your passive capital income. Americans tend to move to Mexico, Panama, Columbia or better still Ecuador, where the US dollar is legal tender. Costa Rica has taken good care of its environment, something that will work in its favour going forward. Land is cheap south of the border and so is the overall cost of living, even if you might have to learn a bit of Spanish to get along.

In Europe, the preferred countries are Spain, Portugal and Malta, presumably for the weather, mainly; the rich and famous prefer Monaco and Liechtenstein. In Asia, Thailand has everything going for it – except a stable political situation. In the Philippines, English is widely used, but the natural environment has been ravaged, as it has in Indonesia; there are still nice places there on some of the more remote islands, but you might need to speak a bit of Bahasa to get by. Malaysia also has super-low cost of living and features high on the best places to retire in international surveys. Although much of the forest is gone and coastal plastic pollution and coral bleaching are serious problems, on the plus-side you have a sympathetic immigration system, with an ideal "Malaysia My Second Home" programme suited for middle-class applicants – you do not have to be a millionaire to qualify.

Are you happy now?

I grew up in one of the happiest countries in the world. But I didn't know it at the time; in fact, I wonder about some of the results from these happiness surveys. The 2018 edition of the World

Happiness Report had Finland on top for the first time, followed by Norway, Denmark, Iceland, Switzerland, Netherlands, Canada, New Zealand, Sweden and Australia.[55]

That survey highlighted a point that might be interesting to would-be immigrants: Happiness is contagious. "The most striking finding of the report is the remarkable consistency between the happiness of immigrants and the locally born," said Professor John Helliwell of Canada's University of British Columbia at the launch of the report. "Although immigrants come from countries with very different levels of happiness, their reported life evaluations converge towards those of other residents in their new countries. Those who move to happier countries gain, while those who move to less happy countries lose."[56]

Notice that all the five Nordic countries are in the top 10. No wonder that Bernie Sanders, during the American presidential primary elections in 2016, singled out Denmark by name as an example of how he would like the US to be. Personally, I am not so sure. When I look at the six criteria used to determine this well-being ranking – income, freedom, trust, healthy life expectancy, social support and generosity – I am missing some other important ones.

How about the weather? I lived for two years in Stavanger, Norway, and that is one rough place, I can tell you. The summer begins in June and ends in July; for the rest of the year it is cold with driving rain; in December it is dark by 3 p.m. All the happy Norwegians flock down to Spain or out to Thailand as soon as they can, to get some much-needed sun. Wouldn't you be happier in a place where you have bright sunshine, the sky is blue and flowers are blooming every day of the year, where a warm rain cools down the site most nights and clears the air, where the water in the pool is always 29°C (84°F). Utopia? Not quite – I live in a place just like that!

How about taxes? In happy Denmark, the tax-to-GDP ratio is 46%, the highest among the OECD countries, according to the

OECD itself.[57] And there is nothing you can do about it. Yes, you can vote at parliamentary elections every fourth year, but that choice is an illusion; although there are currently nine different parties in the legislative assembly, they all more or less have the same platform. They all support the expensive EU bureaucracy, unnecessary NATO regime-change wars, a destructive agricultural policy, as well as lots of money for people who can but do not work. When I lived in Denmark in the 1990s, I found that lack of choice, lack of basic freedoms and human rights to manage your own affairs stifling. Paying 57% income tax and 25% sales tax on top of that may be OK if you are super-rich, but for an ordinary family trying to get by, life in Scandinavia is a struggle.

What about crime? Denmark and Singapore have some 5.7 and 5.6 million people, respectively; the GDP per capita is $53,000 in both places according to World Data Atlas, rounded off to the nearest $1,000. In Denmark, for 2015, there were 63,343 burglaries; in Singapore there were 250 the same year. Rape: 1,051/162. Assault: 1,460/473. Homicide: 56/14.[58] Overall number of reported crime cases in Denmark 2016: 401,407[59]; for Singapore the same year: 32,964.[60] Where would you feel safer and happier?

It's a personal choice

I believe we should take care of our natural environment, as well as the weak in society; we need a strong government to do that. We should build infrastructure, have a good educational system, housing, health, foreign affairs department, help businesses succeed, police our streets, secure our borders and prepare for emergencies. How come Singapore can do all that – in most cases much better than Denmark – and still have a tax-to-GDP ratio of 14%? It is quite simple, really: The government merely keeps communal spending under control. This way, taxation pressure can be kept within reason, leaving members of the public largely free to manage their own affairs.

In Singapore, wage earners are obliged to save a certain share of their income through a compulsory savings scheme called CPF. The idea is that what you make is what you keep, so future retirement benefits as well as healthcare expenses are individually funded. This enables the state to keep other taxes low. Three out of four workers here pay no income tax at all; the rate for the rest starts at 2%, and you have to earn over US$246,000 before the top rate of 22% kicks in. If, for example, you earn US$100,000 per year in chargeable income (i.e. after deductions), you will pay $7,270 income tax.[61] There are no additional local taxes, no taxes on income from interest, dividends or capital gains; the sales tax is 7% (soon to go up to 9%).

I have lived about half my life in each of these countries, Denmark and Singapore. If I ever meet Bernie Sanders I will tell him that he is looking at the wrong role model for modern development. I have voted between the two systems with my feet. I will only leave Singapore if the officers at ICA (the Immigration and Checkpoints Authority) kick me out. My son is a citizen in both countries; he has two passports, but he will have to give up one when he turns 18, as Singapore does not allow dual citizenship. It is his personal choice, but I don't think it will be the Singapore passport that goes into the wastebasket.

5

"Ethics" Is
Many Things

*"Ethics aren't just important in business. They
are the whole point of business."*

— RICHARD BRANSON

We are all in the same boat

So let us assume for a moment that you are somewhat concerned about the state of our planet. In the previous chapters we looked at what is wrong with the environment. But that is not all; there are armed conflicts to be anxious about, poverty, inequality and global health issues that need fixing too. These other concerns are a bit outside the scope of this particular book, however; here I will stick to what I know. I have worked in the resource industry and as a naturalist; I am also a qualified financial analyst and an investor myself, living off my passive income. This is my level of expertise; I am not an authority on global security and certainly not on health matters.

Having said that, I can see why some people would be worried that we are spending too much of our limited resources on activities that do not really improve our welfare and our well-being. It is much better that we talk than we fight; that goes for countries as well as individuals. As people, there is much more that unites us than divides us. I know that, because I have worked in Tanggu

District, China, in Dallas/Fort Worth, Texas, and at safari lodges in East Africa. The world over, people are basically the same; they have pretty much the same desires and aspirations. So why can't we all just get along?

I lived through the Cold War in Europe; it was pretty intense at times. There was a lot of fear-mongering and sabre-rattling on both sides. But it was a triumph for humanity that the transition to democracy within the Soviet bloc – starting with the fall of the Berlin Wall in 1989 – was largely peaceful; only in some of the Baltic states and in Romania was there bloodshed on a serious scale, as far as I remember. I don't agree with violent uprisings or regime-change wars; it is my experience that conflicts are better resolved peacefully over time; the territorial integrity and right to self-determination of nations should be respected. But that is just me, and I accept that other people might have different views.

However, on the whole I think that we can all agree on one thing: We need the earth. We should not wreck it; on the contrary, it is important that we take good care of it. So that will be my focus with regard to capital allocation.

Various values

That we all have the same aspirations in life doesn't mean that we all have the same values. In fact, our values can be quite different, and that is fine as long as they can all be accommodated in a peaceful manner. Take ethical investing. Not only does it mean different things to different groups in society, I would go as far as to say that no two people on Earth have exactly the same attitude to it.

The interest in ethical capital allocation has grown explosively, particularly in the last decade or so, and the growth is accelerating. According to the US SIF – The Forum for Sustainable and Responsible Investment – funds under ethical management in the US grew from $2.71 trillion in 2007 to $3.07 trillion in 2011 and then more than doubled to $8.72 trillion in 2016.[62] Some 20% of assets under management are invested with some regard to SRI (Socially Responsible Investing) and/or ESG (Environmental, Social and Governance) factors. Looking at this globally, a 2016 review by the Global Sustainable Investment Alliance found that $23 trillion of global assets under professional management are under RI (Responsible Investment) strategies, up 25% since 2014. The review concluded: "In relative terms, responsible investment now stands at 26 percent of all professionally managed assets globally. Clearly, sustainable investing constitutes a major force across global financial markets."[63] Please keep in mind that some of these criteria are fairly broad – we will get back to this later in this chapter. But it is sufficient here to establish that ethical investment is a growing trend, a rapidly growing one.

Having studied the subject, it is my view that there are basically two kinds of investors that factor in ethical considerations when they invest. There are those that (A) have sufficiently strong views on ethics so that they simply invest this way to do the right thing. And then there are those that (B) select ethical investments because they firmly believe this to be most profitable. The latter category would agree with Amy Domini, founder and CEO of ethical investment firm Domini Impact Investments, when she says: "To pollute, to discriminate, to violate basic human rights, is just not good for business."[64]

But let us look at the return on capital and general track record of ethical investments a bit later. For now let us dig a bit deeper into the value set of the "A" type of investors, those who invest ethically because they think it is the right thing to do. It is my own observation that there are two sub-types of those. The first consists of ethical liberal investors with progressive (leftist) points of view. Those are often worried about their money being channelled into weapons production, particularly nuclear weapons and also cluster bombs and landmines that kill indiscriminately and litter the battlefield for years after being dropped. Ethical liberals are also likely to be concerned about GMO agriculture; they might be animal rights advocates and/or vegans, and as such they want nothing to do with animal exploitation or consumption. The other sub-type consists of ethical conservatives, maybe with a contrarian or somewhat libertarian view of the world, sceptical of big government. This group could also include a sub-group of Christian or Islamic faith-based investors. They would prioritise family values highly and try to avoid investing in enterprises that promote alcohol, tobacco or offensive entertainment such as pornography or violent videogames. Most likely they would be in the right-to-life camp and would not want to be financing abortion or euthanasia healthcare providers. They might believe in the right to bear arms as well as a strong security apparatus, and as such might be happy to finance arms manufacturers and defence contractors.

With regard to our environment, ethical liberals might resist all further extraction of non-renewable resources, especially fossil fuels. Ethical conservatives might be less concerned about this; they could even be climate change deniers and still have ethical values. Common to the two sub-types – I hope – is a general respect for our natural heritage, a will to conserve what beauty and diversity out there we have left. A basic respect for human rights, decent treatment of all groups and fair business practices should also be universal among all ethical investors.

So what is my view?

As part of my research, I ploughed through a number of books and opinion pieces about these topics – ethical and socially responsible investment. Although somewhat informative, most of it is a tad too broad and vague for my taste; it makes me wonder if these writers have actually tried to invest their own money, ethically or otherwise. I believe that we should be transparent and get everything out on the table. So let me share with you where

I stand on all this. Judging from my sources and my discussions with others regarding the value sets most commonly attributed to ethical investments, I have compiled this table:

Ethical values for negative screening (Author's choice)

Activity to consider	Screen out	Might allow	Don't care
Mining/logging	●		
Road construction		●	
Coal	●		
All fossil fuels		●	
Violations of human rights		●	
Violations of humanitarian principles		●	
Corrupt practices	●		
Nuclear weapons	●		
Landmines	●		
All weapons		●	
GMO agriculture	●		
Pesticide manufacturers	●		
Chemical companies		●	
Meat/dairy/eggs producers		●	
Animal testing		●	
Fur and specialty leather	●		
Gambling/casinos	●		
Tobacco	●		
Violent entertainment		●	
Alcohol		●	
Abortion clinics			●
Pornography		●	

Note that I have chosen "ethical" as the general term for investments where some abstract values are consciously applied in the decision-making. In my classification, "green investing" is a narrower sub-category of ethical investing, where you specifically apply an environmental strategy. SRI can mean Socially Responsible Investing, Sustainable and Responsible Investing or Social Responsible and Impact Investing, depending on who uses the abbreviation. From this chart you can gauge which term fits your priorities best; I will go on using "ethical" to capture them all.

As you can see, I am mostly concerned about our environment. In fact, I am alarmed. As I stated in the opening chapters, I – and many other like-minded observers – believe that we are beyond the point where nature conservation is a niche luxury crusade by a few birdwatchers and tree-huggers. I believe that the loss of natural habitats and pollution from human construction and consumption activities – mainly caused by overpopulation and facilitated by the financial debt culture – is pushing us into an existential crisis. When I look at the facts, the numbers and the events unfolding, in my view they cannot be interpreted any other way.

That is why I aim to avoid financing extractive industries such as mining, and especially coal mining. I am also somewhat concerned about road building into remote areas leading to more habitat destruction, although I appreciate that new roads are sometimes necessary for development. I can accept that some of my funds may be channelled into conventional energy production; I will get back to that in more detail in later chapters. The term "human rights" means many things to many people. In America, a majority of people feel it is a human right to bear arms; others might find that offensive. In general I am personally not too concerned about people; they can and should look after themselves. Would I like to work in a garment factory in Bangladesh, 10 hours a day for $2? No, but I will not prevent others from doing it, if that is their choice. That is why in my portfolio I don't categorically screen out all companies that might be underpaying their workers.

However, there is no excuse (in my view) for corrupt practices, and I also see no value whatsoever in nuclear weapons or other weapons of mass destruction; I want nothing to do with that. Arms in general, conventional weapons? Maybe, maybe not – it might depend on the circumstances. I think that ideally all farming should be organic; but although I find the way most of our meat is produced abhorrent, I am not a vegetarian, so I give food production and trading in general a "Might allow". But not mink, fox and reptile farms – we don't need those. I also see no merit at all in tobacco, and I want nothing to do with gambling. Adult entertainment in general, and booze? I don't have strong views on those; I was young once too, and what consenting adults do is their choice. I still like a margarita or two myself on Friday nights; I see no harm in that! I know that some find abortions unethical and I respect that view, but I don't share it.

So that's my two cents' worth. Feel free to insert your own ticks in the table; it will make it easier for you in the long run if you establish your own explicit values and preferences with regard to where your money should flow.

Capital is shifting

So far this has been mostly about so-called negative screening, i.e. a procedure where you apply your values to screen out – exclude – undesirable investments. But you can also apply positive – inclusive – screening, meaning that you actively seek out investments that you feel are both beneficial and likely to generate return on capital.

Again, this is somewhat subjective, partly because our views differ on what is favourable, and partly because we view the future differently. The secret to successful investing is to spot future trends and participate in the growth. Did he say growth, you might ask? But wasn't it his opinion just before that economic growth has ended? Let me counter that by clarifying that although I and others believe that conventional economic growth – continuously injecting more capital to extract more limited resources – will come to a halt, or has already, I do believe that people will keep on wanting to work. There will be future pockets of activity where capital, labour and productivity combine to generate new value.

You can consider these 10 themes for sustainable investing that Janus Henderson Investors focuses on:[65]

Environmental themes
1. Sustainable transport
2. Water management
3. Efficiency
4. Cleaner energy
5. Environmental services

Social themes
6. Sustainable property and finance
7. Quality of life
8. Health
9. Safety
10. Knowledge and technology

I find this list quite useful for focusing the mind. Later on we will go into more detail about some of these areas. It is sufficient here to establish that these are segments that you could consider for your ethical investments. If you stick to these themes and industries, at least your money will not do a whole lot of harm.

As the world economy approaches the limits of traditional economic growth, capital allocation will have to shift. For instance, as the planet gets more polluted and damaged, we will have to spend more resources on cleaning it up and restoring it. As I write, the Australian government just announced that they will spend

A\$500 million (\$379 million) to restore and protect the Great Barrier Reef; there will be many such projects coming up in the future.[66] In Miami, Florida, they are spending a fortune on raising road levels, new pumps and other flood control measures. In Indonesia, the 32 km Great Garuda sea wall that is planned to protect Jakarta from future flooding will cost no less than US\$40 billion. All this will not really improve our welfare as such, but it will keep a lot of people busy, and for investors there will be some money to be made from return on these investments, unproductive as they might be. Who is going to pick up the plastic in the oceans? Who will clean up the rivers and the lakes, put out the fires and build up some of the bombed-out areas devastated by civil unrest? Find that out, put your money where your mouth is and you might do well going forward.

It's complicated

But as they say, the proof is in the pudding, and here is where the ethics get a bit more complicated. As an investor, you might know that so-called blue-chip companies are large-cap (capitalisation) corporations with a long track record and solid fundamentals. Incidentally, what you might not know is that the term "blue chip" stems from poker, where the blue token is the most valuable; but let us leave that aside here. Here it's important to consider that not many blue-chip companies would pass a thorough investigation into their ethical status. You'll find that there are a lot of grey areas.

Until June 2018, the General Electric Company (GE), listed on the NYSE, was the only company that had been a member of the exclusive Dow Jones Industrial Average index since day one (1896). It has since been taken out of the index, but it is still in the broader S&P 500, so if you buy an ETF linked to that index – and probably many other industrial ETFs – you are bound to own a part of GE. Lately GE has had a bit of a hard time, its share price dropping from $32 per share in 2016 to $13 in 2018. But apart from that, the company is consistently ranked as one of the most admired in the world (by *Fortune* magazine), one of the best places to work (by the Human Rights Campaign Foundation) and yes, as one of the most ethical. Every year, *Ethisphere Magazine* honours the 135 most ethical companies, covering millions of employees and trillions of dollars of market cap.[67] GE was on that list in 2018 and indeed the company does make some wind turbines and they do have a healthcare division – both noble undertakings. But most of their revenue is derived from conventional power generation, oil and gas, aviation and transportation. So would you screen a company like that in or out?

With regard to human rights, the Human Rights Campaign Foundation also ranks Raytheon Company as one of the best places to work in America.[68] Right, it is a great place to work if you like to make nuclear-capable cruise missiles and depleted-uranium munitions. Several lawsuits have been filed against Raytheon for contaminating the environment. Northrop Grumman Corporation and Lockheed Martin Corporation are two other wonderful places to work – from a human rights standpoint – according to that foundation; maybe not so wonderful for the humans exposed to their B-2 bombers and Trident thermonuclear missiles. Would you buy their shares? Be my guest; I wouldn't. But if I want to own a share of the innovative and productive American economy and purchase an ETF linked to the S&P 500 index, that is exactly what I will end up doing, i.e. buy into all these defence contractors. Do you see what I mean? Ethical investing has a lot of grey areas.

Buying and owning shares in blue-chip companies is like walking through a minefield for an ethical investor: you constantly have to watch where you step. If you are based in Singapore like I am, you might want to know that only one company listed on the Singapore Exchange (SGX) made it into *Ethisphere Magazine*'s 2018 list of most ethical corporations: Singapore Telecommunications

Ltd, our largest and government-linked phone company. That is nice for Singtel, but where does that leave all the other companies listed here? Those you will have to judge for yourself.

You could check out the list of companies scoring high in sustainability, as compiled by the Toronto-based research firm Corporate Knights. The firm uses 17 indicators relating to environmental, social and governance (ESG) aspects and compares some 5,994 companies from various industries. Although "sustainable" is probably one of the most poorly defined and overused terms in business – right next to "eco" – this list might give you some idea which companies are generally well run and pleasant to be associated with. In Singapore in 2018, Singtel made it into the list, followed by CapitaLand and City Developments, two property developers; the previous year StarHub – another telco – also made it in.[69]

You can check out the whole list of so-called sustainable companies at the Corporate Knights website, but if I were you I would not put too much emphasis on it.[70] The list is a who's-who of corporate players like Nestlé, Merck, Siemens, BMW, Samsung and all the usual corporate giants, many linked to oil, cosmetics, cars, etc. Are they the ones that are going to save the world? Didn't we just establish that continuous burning of fossil fuels is not sustainable? Then you can check the internet and search for Nestlé: "Why Nestlé is one of the most hated companies in the world", one article says.[71] The company has been linked to child labour, unethical promotions, consumer manipulation, pollution, price-fixing and mislabelling. I hope they don't sustain all those practices, if that is really the case. I don't know enough about this particular company to evaluate them, but I do know that things are not always as they appear, so use your own critical judgement before you invest.

Or maybe – for Singapore specifically – you can use the Sustainable Business Awards Singapore (SBA) to guide you.[72] Each year the corporate bigwigs put on their suits to gather and dine in style and give each other awards. The winners are the usual suspects of property development, banking and industry; among the 2017 winners for Indonesia was Asia Pulp and Paper (APP). That particular company has been heavily implicated in deforestation and the Southeast Asian haze crisis of 2015; that year the major supermarkets in Singapore decided to boycott all APP products.[73] The tag-line on the SBA website is: "We cannot choose between economic growth and sustainability – we must have both." I know one person who would disagree with that: the old-timer American ecological economist Herman Daly. Daly firmly believes that such a statement is a contradiction in terms; conventional economic expansion in a confined space cannot by definition be sustainable. If you are inclined to, check out some of Daly's papers and interviews by googling "steady state economy".

By the way, the big banks winning sustainability awards? With regard to the financing of the extractive economy, much of what takes place is of course a bank/client privilege; we simply don't know what is going on. But some cases see the light of day. In 2016 it was reported that widespread rainforest clearance and burning by the Rajawali Group in Kalimantan, Indonesia, was financed not only by a US$192 million loan from government-linked Bank Negara Indonesia but also with funds from Credit Suisse and Bank of America. According to NGOs studying this, more than a third of the $43 billion in loans and underwritings linked to companies engaged in deforestation and forest burning in Southeast Asia alone comes from American, European and Japanese banks – many of which have sustainability pledges that specifically mention deforestation. Bank Negara Indonesia itself has a sustainability policy that says that its clients must adopt "minimum environmental, social and governance standards". Andrew Mitchell with the Global Canopy Programme said on that occasion: "Destroying the world's forests makes fighting climate change almost impossible. The finance sector is really lagging behind in realising that."[74]

Ah, but at least the green, humanitarian Scandinavians and their banking systems are in the clear, right? Don't bet on it. The money trail is a winding one, and it reaches far. "While Nordic governments have taken a strong public stance against deforestation, major banks and pension funds in the region – including the Norwegian government's own pension fund – have invested more than US$2 billion in six Southeast Asian banks that finance more than 50 percent of Indonesia's rainforest-ravaging oil palm operations" – so said a report released in 2017 by Rainforest Foundation Norway.[75] The report concluded: "Southeast Asian backers of palm oil production that are key recipients of Nordic investments include Indonesia's four largest banks and two from Singapore, OCBC and DBS Bank. The four Indonesian banks account for half of all lending supporting palm oil production in Indonesia, with some US$12.5 billion in outstanding loans. The Singapore banks do not publish details of their palm oil investments, but other sources, including financial records from 16 publicly-traded Indonesian palm oil companies, revealed OCBC and DBS were among the industry's largest lenders." Hey, wait a minute, I am a shareholder in OCBC, where does that leave me?

Finding smaller targets

All in all, it seems that virtually every big corporation out there is in on it, the environmental degradation. And yet, most of them claim to be ethical and sustainable. It doesn't matter if they deal in nuclear weapons, tobacco or palm oil, they will all have fancy mission statements in their annual reports paying lip service to ESG and sustainability goals. This is alright, lip service is a lot better than no service at all; but for the ethical investor, this spinning of facts goes on till it is your head that spins, and it becomes difficult to separate the grain from the chaff. These days, all corporations have an environmental department and officers employed to deal with sustainability issues; they go for training courses in GRI reporting – Global Reporting Initiative – and learn how to make fancy reports and powerpoint presentations to tweak the message of the company; a whole support industry has evolved around this, offering platforms and tuition in greenwashing.

The large corporations take on all this partly to address and comply with new legislation from governments or from the stock exchange where they are listed – for example, since 2016 the SGX in Singapore has required all listed companies to publish a yearly sustainability report. But partly they also do it to fend off possible public criticism and to qualify to attend all the various sustainability conferences that make them look good. Here their staff join the growing multitude of "conference-hoppers", as Naomi Klein calls them, the men and women in suits and power-outfits who travel the globe on business class to meet and tell each other how hard they work to look after the environment. It is one big happy family of corporations, NGOs and government departments; they all speak the same language: that things are worrying, but soon we will have this problem licked, and then we can all go back to normal and grow and consume like we always have.

So, what is an investor to do to cut through this haze of sustainability chatter? There are several strategies you can apply. First of all, look at what the company does, not what it says. Next, you can tweak your principles a bit. Maybe you have to accept that this is not a perfect world; if you want your money to grow, you might have to lower your standards somewhat. Look long and hard at your ethics spreadsheet above and swallow some of your pride. Negatively screen out those companies that you definitely don't like, but accept others even though they play multiple roles in the economy. That could be industrial conglomerates like GE or Siemens that both contribute to global warming as well as environmental improvement; in Singapore a company like Sembcorp Industries would fall into that category. What about the banks? They all quite likely provide financing to some companies you might not want to support, but what can you do about that? Most investors would not like to be shut off entirely from the whole financial sector, which in general has been quite profitable for the last 10 years or so, thank you very much. Personally I don't think I will divest the few shares I have in OCBC anytime soon, but I will keep these issues in mind!

Another strategy is to move away from the blue-chips. You could try to identify smaller-cap companies that you really like. There are many that are exclusively involved in only one of the 10 ethical themes that we identified earlier. This would require a bit more research; but if you are up to it, this active capital management approach could be interesting and profitable. That way you would not have to contend with large corporations that you don't sympathise with. Just keep in mind that the risk in dealing with small-cap companies and start-ups with yet unproven business models is considered significantly greater. In the next chapter we will look in more detail at how you can position yourself this way and mitigate the risks.

Use the power of capital

If you think you are the only one struggling to reconcile your ethical values with your money, don't fret, you are not alone. With our economy structured the way it is, to make money you have to wreck the earth. Traditionally, the successful people living in big houses and driving big cars all worked in the oil business or they dug coal and minerals out of the ground. Or they had big cattle ranches. In Asia they were tin miners or cleared the forest to plant rubber and pineapple and palm oil. The tin miners went into banking, insurance, construction, car dealerships – you name it – and gradually they covered what was left of the habitat with roads and houses and offices and shopping centres. You cannot make any money just by leaving things the way they are, by conserving stuff – where is the profit in that?

People who had other values had the choice of either tagging along or dropping out of the mainstream economy altogether and accepting that they would always be at the bottom of the ladder, like some hippies and back-to-nature freaks did, camping in the woods, rejecting money and growing their own food. Personally I don't accept that choice, and I believe it is becoming increasingly less relevant. Maybe I am a bit of a cynic, but I believe that no one out there is going to help you; you have to help yourself. I just want to be free, and if that means participating for a while in the extractive economy, so be it. In our nature group here in Singapore, we have several oil field engineers; I was one once, too. Who said anything about global warming? We have a member who worked for most of his life selling steel blades to the timber industry; he would travel to the sawmills on Sumatra and deliver them tools to cut up the forest. In his spare time he would study rainforest animals and work for their conservation.

In *Conscious Money* (2012), Patricia Aburdene quotes Cliff Feigenbaum saying about this strategy: "That's like profiting from tobacco stocks during the day and contributing to the American Cancer Society at night." There is some truth in that, but I am sure that veteran SRI investor Feigenbaum would agree that maybe not everyone is as privileged as he is, making a good ethical living as publisher of *Green Money Journal*. Out in the real world, most people just try to get by doing whatever job is available. Like the arms dealer said: You have to make a living.

If that is the reality for you, don't fight it, and don't feel guilty about it. But use the money you accumulate from extraction work and save it; don't squander it on frivolous consumption that increases the demand for yet more extraction. I quoted Dieter Helm in Chapter 3 and suggested a similar strategy for both governments and individuals: Conserve the financial capital generated from natural habitat loss and use it to protect, restore and rebuild our natural capital foundation. That should be our way forward.

As an investor, use the same strategy. Don't fritter away your money; first of all make it grow. If that means owning a few profitable bank stocks, so be it. Even Naomi Klein (*This Changes Everything*, 2014) admits as much: "Capitalism threatens our existence… but that doesn't mean savvy investors can't get very rich on the way down, both from the final scramble for fossil fuels, and by setting themselves up as disaster capitalists." If you are poor, you are no good to anyone, you are powerless. But as and when you can, support those enterprises and individuals who work to improve our earth. Who knows, you might even make a dollar that way. Today there are a lot more opportunities out there for ethical investors, and in this book we will be identifying some of the most promising ones.

The green tycoons

Staying with Klein, she has a wonderful chapter in her book in which she considers the efforts of people like Richard Branson, Michael Bloomberg and Bill Gates to save the earth, and she documents how they mainly fell flat. In 2006, Branson pledged to spend roughly $3 billion over the following decade to develop biofuels as an alternative to oil and gas, and other technologies to battle climate change; seven years into that pledge, less than 10% of that sum was committed, and the idea appeared to peter out into the sand. During the same period, Branson's Virgin group of airlines went on an airline-procurement spree, and the company's greenhouse gas emissions soared by 40–177%, depending on the destinations. Meanwhile Branson unveiled Virgin Racing to compete in Formula One motor sports and invested heavily in Virgin Galactic to bring passengers on completely pointless but energy-consuming space trips. I am sure that Branson is a good person who really means well; it just seems that the old ways of doing things are simply still too profitable to resist.

The same could be said for another green Messiah: Elon Musk.

Musk has repeatedly declared that his goal in life is to change the world for the better, fight global warming and reduce the risk of human extinction. On paper, Musk is a multi-billionaire; the only problem is that his main company Tesla Inc does not actually make any money and is $10 billion in debt. His electric cars are heavily dependent on government subsidies to sell, but when the LTA (Land Transport Authority of Singapore) tested a Tesla Model S in 2016, they found that it actually drew twice as much power from the grid as what was specified by Tesla and in that way polluted more than a petrol-powered Mercedes E-class, considering that power in Singapore is generated from fossil fuels.[76] This was confirmed independently in Hong Kong, where the Tesla S was found to pollute more than a BMW 320i.[77] Like I said earlier, things are not always as they appear. Yet, Tesla's market cap at around $50 billion is larger than Ford Motor's ($43 billion), although Ford made 6.4 million vehicles in 2016, while Tesla made 76,000. Go figure!

Another one of Elon Musk's companies is of course SpaceX, flying high on contracts from NASA (i.e. the government, again) and defence companies. Musk is planning a manned mission to Mars in 2025; he wants to set up a colony there by 2033. Maybe he agrees with Stephen Hawking when the latter said during a speech in 2017 that our time on Earth would be limited to just 100 more years due to overpopulation and global warming: "We are running out of space and the only place to go is other worlds. It is time to explore other solar systems. I am convinced that humans need to leave Earth."[78]

Did I read this right, "other solar systems"? I may not be as smart as Musk or Hawking, but I do know that travelling to other solar systems is not an option for us. Where did that idea come from? The nearest solar system to ours is Alpha Centauri and it is 4.2 light years away. Even other planets in our own system – it is not going to happen. Move 8 billion people to Mars, just 3 light minutes away at its closest? When Earth and Mars line up correctly – which is once every 26 months – the one-way trip out takes around 10 months. Honestly, I don't think there will be tickets for everyone, do you? Why don't we try and use our limited resources to take care of what we have already got? Our own beautiful, unique green-blue planet – or what is left of it.

That doesn't mean that we should give up entirely on the green tycoons; in fact, we need them badly. In the future we will depend on wealthy private individuals to pitch in and save the earth; we cannot always expect or wait for governments to do the right thing. In 2018, Michael Bloomberg lost patience with the US public administration dragging their feet on the environment, and he decided to give $4.5 million out of his own pocket to cover the government's share of expenses to get the Paris climate accord implemented.[79] In *Eco Barons* (2009), Edward Humes provides a lot of such inspiring case studies, and I could come up with many more from my own experience, of people of means who helped out, sometimes in little ways, other times big.

One of the largest ethical contributors ever is Ted Turner – the American media tycoon and founder of CNN who was famously married to Jane Fonda for a while. Turner is concerned about mainly two things: nuclear war and environmental collapse caused by global warming. To prevent wars and armed conflicts, he donated a round $1 billion to the UN back in 1997 – to be paid in instalments over 10 years. At the time Turner said that his net worth was $3.2 billion, and he could get by fine with just $2.2 billion; that makes good sense to me. With regard to nature conservation, Turner has turned himself into one of the largest land owners in America; he preserves what little pristine wilderness is left out West by simply buying it up. Then he releases bison on the land, that old iconic American mammal. Turner has the largest herd of bison in the world and owns a chain of bison meat restaurants to manage the population.

The Asian way

Where are the Asians in all this? And the other emerging market economies? I have heard it so many times here in Asia: You in the West are so rich, you can afford to be ethical. We in Asia are poor, we are still struggling; we don't have the luxury of taking care of our environment, let alone the planet as a whole. People in the West must cut down on their consumption and CO_2 pollution, while we expand ours to catch up.

There is a grain of truth in this. I looked at Denmark as a case study earlier on, since this small country is often elevated to a role model by greenies and liberals. Correct, Denmark ruined their original habitat long ago. Just like how Malaysia and Indonesia were until recently covered in lush tropical rainforest, Denmark used to be almost entirely covered in old hardwood oak forest. The Vikings cut much of that down to build houses and ships during the Viking Age, around 700–1000 AD. Most of the rest went during the reign of King Christian IV in the 17th century. For what? You guessed it: warships, and most of them were sunk by navies from neighbouring countries during futile wars anyway. For the last 400 years or so, Denmark has been doing fine with hardly any of its natural habitat left standing; the forests found there now are just monotonous beech and spruce plantations. Yet, Denmark has prospered. So why can't we in Asia?

First of all, don't forget that Asia has actually done quite well for itself since the 1950s and 60s, when most countries in Southeast Asia gained their independence. The Swiss financial analyst Marc Faber points out in one of his interviews that Asia has grown much more rapidly during the last few decades than have Europe and America. Asia is indeed catching up. It is not that the West is really declining, but relatively they are, as wages stagnate there, while the middle class in Asia expands. It has been called "the great convergence" by some observers. During a presentation in India in 2018, Dr Faber said that "the end of Western economic and political hegemony" is coming, and Asia's rise to the top is virtually unstoppable.[80] This is a projection of middle-class inhabitants in the three largest Asian countries up to the year 2030:

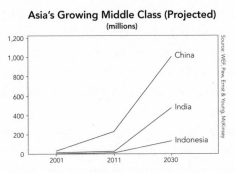

Asia's Growing Middle Class (Projected)
(millions)

Before you get carried away by all the current debate about global inequality, consider this chart as well, which shows the increase in GDP per capita in three areas: the whole world, the former communist bloc – which started to take off this century after a consolidation period following the fall of the Berlin Wall in 1989 – and then finally the developing countries, all this since the year I got my driver's licence, i.e. in just one lifetime.

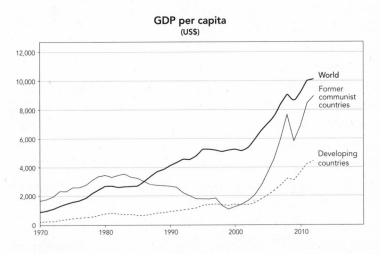

GDP per capita
(US$)

Personally I would take the numerical values on the Y-axis of this chart with a grain of salt. The bloated expansion of the GDP in the West has not done much to improve actual quality of life; much of this is simply due to monetary expansion, and most of the wealth has been concentrated among a small minority of the population that was already rich. So these larger numbers don't necessarily mean that the world is doing well; throughout much of the world, the Genuine Progress Indicator (GPI) shows little improvement. That is why the millions of refugees pouring into America and Europe all have nice clothes and the latest smartphones with them, even as their places of origin are breaking down in poverty and violence and rapidly becoming uninhabitable. What the chart shows, however, is the relative convergence between regions.

So, now that Asia is (almost) as rich as the West – or getting that way – the old mantra that the people there don't have to take care of the environment does not really hold water any longer. And secondly, this time it is different, as they say, it really is. When King Christian IV destroyed the last of the Danish forests around 1610, there were still plenty of nice habitats left in other places to gobble up. When Europeans ran out of resources at home, they just raided the rest of the world. But guess what, we don't have that option anymore. The world is full – full of people and full of man-made stuff. There are no more empty continents and vast wide-open spaces we can expand into.

In Denmark – and, I suspect, most other Western countries – nature conservation and green policies are imposed and controlled in a rather top-down manner. For example, in 2017 only 1,240 electric and hybrid vehicles were sold in Denmark (about 0.6% of the total); that is less than in any of the other Nordic countries, including tiny Iceland, where around 3,000 were sold.[81] Why so few, especially since hybrid cars are great in today's dense traffic? Because hybrid cars are not subsidised in Denmark, so they cost more. Like in most other places, people in Denmark love to be

What is the Genuine Progress Indicator?

Usually we measure our society's economic progress with the GDP, the Gross Domestic Product, and we equate that with quality of life and life satisfaction – higher GDP is good, lower GDP is bad. But the problem with that is that the GDP captures *all* economic activity. This way, the catastrophic Deepwater Horizon oil spill in the Gulf of Mexico in 2010 added billions of dollars to the American GDP, but really added nothing but misery to the people in that area. Natural disasters, crime, resource depletion, deforestation, loss of wetlands, noise/water/air pollution, family breakdowns, traffic accidents, commuting... these activities add to the GDP, but actually make our lives worse. That is why life satisfaction in a country like the UK has increased very little since 1973, while the GDP has exploded.

Enter the GPI, the Genuine Progress Indicator. This index is designed to filter out negative contributions to the GDP; I mention a few above, others are inequality, lost leisure time and consumer durables costs. On the positive side, the GPI adds the value of some activities not usually captured by GDP statistics such as volunteer work and domestic labour. All in all, 26 positive as well as negative factors are incorporated into the GPI. Calculated this way, a chart showing both the GDP and the GPI for the US in year 2000 dollar value would look like this – while the GDP tripled since the 1970s, the GPI barely moved:

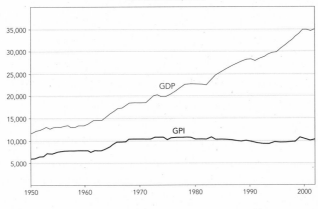

green... only not so much when it costs extra! In Norway – where there are massive financial incentives to buy EVs – a third of all cars sold are either electric or plug-in hybrids. In this particular country (Norway), EVs actually make some sense, and that is because most of the juice in the grid comes from renewable sources, mainly hydroelectric power. But would they sell without state subsidies? I doubt it.

Plastic bags? In Danish supermarkets it costs DKK3.50 to collect one (about US$0.60 each); surprise... not many are collected; most people bring their own bags. A bus ride across Copenhagen costs between US$4.00 and US$17.85 depending on distance; within Singapore it is between US$0.60 for a short trip and US$1.55 for a cross-island journey. I have a nagging suspicion that is why you see so many people on bicycles in Copenhagen, even in the rain and the snow. Recycling? In Denmark you are refunded between DKK1 and DKK3 per bottle/can you bring in for recycling; so most bottles are reused, and kids and pensioners will collect them for the reward. How many bottles would be returned without this deposit is anyone's guess; but mine would be... zero? In 2017, the Danish daily *Jyllandsposten* reported that two-thirds of Danes expressed the view that air travel is an environmental problem, when asked during a survey conducted by KLM Royal Dutch Airlines. Yet, when asked what makes them chose an airline, price – not the sustainability policy – made the difference. And when asked if they expect to fly less in the future, the Danes replied no; in fact they have never flown around the world as much as they do right now.

The world likes to have some role models, and often Denmark is put out as a green model for the rest of the world to follow. We want to think that surely there must be someone out there who gets it right. But 301 leading earth scientists in Denmark do not agree with this assessment, that development in that country is environmentally sustainable. They co-published an op-ed in the Danish paper *Politiken* in May 2018 with the statement (my own translation): "We Danes are among the worst (environmental) offenders. That is because the average Dane's CO_2 footprint is among the highest in the world."[82] The distinguished authors pointed out that this is because the average Danish shopper is a major consumer of beef, electronics and clothes, and because the large transport sector is almost entirely dependent on petrol, jet-fuel, diesel and dirty bunker fuels for the shipping industry. "The total CO_2 emissions from all economic activities haven't fallen since the 1990s... Our high CO_2 emissions mean that the story about Denmark as a 'green' country must be taken with great reservations." The authors point out that to really make a difference, the Danes should go car-free, stop flying and eat less meat. None of that is happening at the moment.

My point is: Yes, as I have mentioned, there are some success stories up in the north. Nature conservation societies attract a lot of members, there are some isolated inspirational developments; I mentioned the plastic clean-up in the North Sea, later I will point out the Danish use of sustainable power for electricity generation. And yes, there are strong hierarchical institutions in place to effectively design and enforce selected green policies; lip service is paid to the environment at all the international conference-hopper meetings. But when it comes to consumption patterns, economic choices and general lifestyle, are Danes, Scandinavians, Westerners in general better than others? Maybe not.

It does help the local environment of course that the Scandinavians outsource most of their dirty consumption. When I grew up in Denmark in the 1950s, virtually all of our stuff was made locally, including clothes, tools, bicycles, ships, toys – and even the batteries that went into them. The shipyards have all closed, and I don't think there are many AA battery factories in Denmark today; all that nasty stuff is made somewhere else. Think of the mess that country would be if the Danes had to dig up their own rare earth minerals somewhere and put them into phones and computers. Or dye their own cloth and dump the wastewater in a river nearby to keep prices competitive. They get others to do all that horrible business for them; but the Danes love the low prices and the sheer abundance of cheap stuff filling up their shopping centres. China and India can devastate their countries, to the point where people riot in the streets because their neighbourhoods become uninhabitable. In the meantime, the Danes get rich writing computer programmes in nice heated offices, which doesn't generate so much filth. Well-paid Danish experts travel out to Third World countries and provide ecological consulting services and advise on environmental restoration techniques; i.e. they make a fortune telling others how to clean up after the disaster they caused in the first place.

But that is just the way it turned out; the emerging market economies benefited too – from becoming the factories of the world and from global trade. Everyone was a winner... no, sorry, not everyone: The earth suffered, as did those who depend on it. Now we have to think differently. So if Asians like the Western way of life and Western technologies, blue jeans and the Western standard of living, we would all expect them to also accept Western-led initiatives to save the earth. Even better, Asia should take the lead and move into the forefront of ethical and SRI investment policies. As a matter of fact, this would align well with traditional Eastern thinking. In his paper "Confucian Ethics and the Environment", Confucius expert Li Tianchen writes: "Taking the Confucian view that the current ecological crisis stems from the spiritual crisis in human beings, the solution to the ecological crisis ultimately rests with the spiritual regeneration of human beings. In the final analysis, to protect nature and the environment is to protect human beings themselves... to the benefit of generations still unborn. The time is opportune to realise ecological harmony through Confucian ethics in this 'greening' century."[83]

In the next chapter we will look more closely at the practicalities of how you can "realise ecological harmony" by positioning yourself financially in an ethical manner.

6

Position Yourself

*"Until things are brighter,
I'm the Man In Black."*
— JOHNNY CASH

Am I too gloomy?

I had a good friend and colleague when I was working in the oil business, an American petroleum engineer from Austin, Texas. Once, we were flying out of Aberdeen, Scotland, for a job off the coast of Cork, Ireland, when the plane started shaking violently. I said in jest: "Richard, we are going to crash!" But Richard didn't think it was funny. He turned to me and told me sternly that if I ever said something like that again, he would tell Joe (our operations manager) never to send the two of us out together again. My friend believed firmly that by thinking aloud and verbalising problems and disasters, you could make them happen.

I don't think so, but a lot of people do. I see commentators out there urging the public to think positive thoughts, to look on the bright side, to be optimistic. Is the glass half-full or is it half-empty? Those in the half-full camp cherry-pick data to show that things are not so bad. I cherry-pick information too, i.e. I select data points to make my narrative more vivid. But just the fact that there are so many bad studies to pick from is in itself alarming to me. I don't think the glass is half-empty; I think we are running on the fumes. We cannot avoid the troubles ahead by collectively ignoring them and thinking happy thoughts; that's not going to fix anything. We have to identify the threats ahead, discuss them out in the open, focus on the risks and find solutions. It doesn't have to be depressing to think that way. To me it is more miserable if you sweep the dangers under the carpet, only to be confronted with them later when you are not prepared.

I take some comfort in the fact that I am not the only one with that attitude. Try to find that great song by Johnny Cash that I quote from above; he wrote it in 1971 during the Vietnam War.[84] Like Cash, I don't mind if I have to "carry off a little darkness on my back", if it will help.

But let us return to the practicalities of investing in an ethical manner. It is easy to be a bit disillusioned with the whole ethical thing. Like: Will my actions really make a difference? And: Why should I risk my money to save the earth, when everyone else is getting rich wrecking it? First of all, yes, what each one of us does really will make a difference. Each time you spend a dollar in the supermarket you change something. If you buy an ethical product, good people get your money; if you buy some GMO junk stuffed with addictive corn syrup, other people will get it (let me leave it at that). And that goes for your investment decisions as well. Lots of surveys show that if you do the right thing and help others and help the earth, you will feel better about yourself and be happier overall. Secondly, you can make money without wrecking the earth; in fact it is easier today than ever before. That is because there are many more options available for ethical investors compared to just a decade ago, and then because the sentiment among both consumers and financiers has changed recently. The current trend is clearly towards ethical capital allocation; and if you believe in the mantra "the trend is your friend", go with it. You just need to study how to do it.

Bonds versus stocks

I will not go into all the details of how to set up an ordinary profitable investment portfolio, since I have already done so! My book
Be Financially Free covers all that; you just need to tweak those
skills to incorporate the ethical standards that we're looking at in
this volume.

It should be sufficient here to reiterate a few key concepts,
just enough for you to get started on your ethical investment jour-
ney. The most important one is the difference between bonds and
stocks. When you buy bonds you are a loaner; when you buy stocks
you are an owner. Bonds are so-called fixed income products; the
investor in reality provides a loan to the issuer; as a reward he is
paid interest, a fixed coupon rate. When the bond matures, the
bond holder is paid back all his money, the principal; before maturity the bond can be traded on the open bond market. Let us say
a $100 bond pays a yearly coupon of $5; if the investor buys at par
– $100 – the yield is of course 5/100 = 5% p.a. If the investor gets
the bond at a lower price, say $80, the yield will be higher, in this
case 5/80 = 6.25% p.a. This way the bond market is sensitive to
the overall interest rate levels; as rates go up, bond prices tend to
decline, and vice versa.

There are two major types of bonds in the fixed income
market: sovereign debt and corporate credit. In the US, the federal
government issues Treasury bonds, the state and local authorities
municipal debt; in the UK this product is called gilts. In Singapore,
government bonds such as SSBs (Singapore Savings Bonds) are
issued periodically to stimulate the local bond market and provide
safe security products for retail investors. Bond yields vary for each
product and depend mainly on maturity; the yield is usually higher
for longer maturities, but not always. If the yield is lower for "long
end" bonds (like 10–30 years' maturity) than for short duration
bonds (1–5 years), the yield curve is said to be inverted, and this
typically signals that a recession has started or is under way.

Corporations also issue bonds to finance their operations, in more perverse cases also to buy back their own shares or continue paying dividends. While sovereign debt in stable countries is considered risk-free – i.e. the interest rate on short-maturity bonds is regarded as the so-called risk-free rate that is used in calculations to analyse the performance of capital management operations – this is not the case for corporate bonds. Unlike a country, a private company can go belly up; the risk of that happening is evaluated by credit rating agencies. If a company's bonds are rated between AAA (triple A) and BBB (triple B) they are considered investment grade; below that – i.e. BB down to D for default – they are considered "junk". Yes, that is the actual term used in financial jargon! Corporate credit will always provide a better yield than sovereign debt; investors simply demand a higher return for the increase in risk. Junk bonds sell at lower prices still, i.e. even higher yield.

Should a private company go bust, it might file for bankruptcy for a period while it tries to restructure and continue operations. If that fails, it will be wound up, liquidated. In that case, the bond holders will get what money is left in the company after staff and suppliers have been paid. Most likely shareholders will get nothing. So, in general, equities carry a higher risk than do bonds.

The sovereign bond market is of little interest to the ethical investor; government bonds are essentially just a safe way to park some of your money for a while. Corporate bonds could have an ethical element to them. When you buy the debt of a company, you are providing capital for their operations, so you are supporting them and assisting in their endeavours.

To keep this simple and for the sake of clarity, the following discussion will relate primarily to equity investments.

Shares, stocks and equity are terms for the same thing: They are certificates of part-ownership of a private company. Shares don't have an expiry date like most bonds; you can hold on to them for as long as the business is up and running. You can buy shares over the counter from another shareholder, but most likely you will invest in a listed company that has its shares traded on a stock exchange. Occasionally, when a private limited company "goes public" it will sell its shares in a so-called IPO – initial public offering – at a fixed price set by the company and the underwriting financial institution. But after that, the price will swing up and down, as the demand for the shares from investors fluctuates.

Investing or trading

To buy and sell shares you must have a middleman – either a stockbroker or an online trading platform that will execute your trades for you. All this is as easy as pie to set up. What is a lot harder is selecting the right companies and providing yourself with a reliable and continuous passive income as well as capital appreciation.

If you get a bank to help you, the bank will assign a broker to you and the shares you buy will be registered in your name. This is a bit expensive, as most banks charge a fee of around 0.5% commission on each purchase; but if you don't want to trade – i.e. buy and sell the shares frequently – that is fine. This strategy is called buy-and-hold: you carefully select companies you like and hold on to them for years. You just sit back and do very little; any dividends will be credited to your current account in the bank.

This tactic is too cumbersome and too expensive if you want to trade frequently. For that you need to find an online trading platform and execute the trades yourself. There are many of such platforms; check their terms and costs or speak to your friends before you pick one. I will refrain from making any recommendations here; it depends on where you are and what exactly you need to do. For Singapore, valuepenguin.sg has a shortlist of recommended brokers in this country and a catalogue of all the others, with their terms and fees listed.[85] For more advice, you can also join an online investment chat-group if you like that sort of thing

– you know: "Hey, Bro... what do I do??" There are tons of those. But in general, expect to pay very low trading fees, probably just 0.12–0.20% or so, with a minimum of perhaps $10 per transaction or even less.

Now you have access to a mind-boggling selection of stocks, bonds, funds, currencies, futures, options and other derivatives. With the platform I use, I can buy and sell shares on 39 different stock exchanges around the world, i.e. thousands and thousands of listed companies. That is not counting all the ETFs, FX and derivative products also available. But personally I like to keep things simple, otherwise you get overwhelmed by information overload. So let us just stick to the basic stock-picking action here for now. Your online broker will use a trustee company to deposit your holdings; that means you will still receive dividend payments and corporate action notifications – such as stock splits and mergers – but because you are not the registered owner of the shares, you will not be invited to AGMs. Not receiving the annual report from "your" company is no great loss these days – it is always easy to find online. But for investors concerned with the ethics of a corporation, not having access to the AGM could be a negative. Active ethical owners might want to attend the AGM and confront the management of the company with questions about the ethics of operations, so keep this in mind if it is important to you.

Do you need advice? That is really up to you. Sarah Pennells (*Green Money*, 2009) recommends that you seek advice, and she might be right. However, she is based in the UK where there is a boatload of financial advisers available who specialise in ethical investing. Here in Asia, it might be harder to find one. If you do engage an adviser, have a talk with him or her before you sign on the dotted line. Make sure her credentials are satisfactory, and that she understands what you want to do. Also check the fee structure and get an idea about how much the advice will set you back. Maybe try an online robo-adviser; it is a new trend that is still in the development phase, but it might be worth looking into. In *Be Financially Free*, I go into the issue of insurance in more detail, and I explain why I think you should never buy any insurance at all – life insurance or otherwise – if your aim is to be financially free. If you cut out the insurance bit, and do some home study on securities investments, I believe it is possible for you to manage your nest egg yourself.

Analytical tools

In Chapter 9 we will look in more detail at what an ethical invest-ment portfolio might look like. For now it will suffice to stress that this is where your ethical standards come into play, when you pick stocks. Only you can decide what is right for you. Like I said, I don't think there are two people in the world with exactly the same values. Our ethics are as individually different as our fingerprints, eye structure and facial features!

You don't want to wreck the earth, but you also don't want to lose your hard-earned savings – I can sympathise with that. Let us say you have applied positive/negative screening across the stock exchange where you are engaged, leaving you with a shortlist of target companies that you might invest in. You look at those more closely from an ethical point of view: Which companies do you really like, and how much mixed activity will you tolerate? Say you love all animals and hate meat producers; would you invest in a supermarket chain that derives, say, 10% of their revenue from meat? You might screen that one out, or you might close one eye if you otherwise really like the company. Only you will know what is right for you.

Now that you have your final list of targets, your trading platform can probably help you with some of the screening and organise this register for you. But how do you pick the right ones before you hit that "Buy" key? This process will not be much differ-ent from what any other investor would do: Here you are looking for the best yield and overall return on capital. In a nutshell, you identify the sector you like, say clean energy or health – areas with growth potential, even in a stagnating economy. Then you look at the individual companies within that sector and apply the usual investment analysis.

Most importantly there is the PE, the Price/Earnings ratio, i.e. the current stock price over latest earnings (not paid-out dividends, but company profits). It is sometimes expressed as forward earnings, with next year's earnings estimate as the denominator. Low is good, high is not so good. Keep in mind that this factor does not work so well for growth companies. Last time I checked, Amazon had a PE ratio of 237 – that is astronomical! Yet, I know people who have made good money on this stock, and many experts still recommend it as a buy, even at this staggering multiple. But Apple Inc now has a PE of 17, which roughly means that you are likely to make your money back in 17 years – doesn't that sound like a safer bet?

Also check EPS (earnings per share), Dividend Payout Ratio, P/B ratio (Price-to-Book) – the terms should be self-explanatory or you can consult my 2016 book for details. Look at not only how much income and expenses the company has, but also at the balance sheet; check for excessive levels of unsecured debt and the gearing ratio such as D/E, the debt-to-equity ratio, which preferably should be lower than 1. You can find these variables and many more in various places. Your stock exchange probably has them online for listed companies; otherwise just check Yahoo, Bloomberg or one of the other financial sites. If you are more serious, go into the annual report of the company itself. Look at its latest financial statements and perform a more detailed fundamental analysis of the company, if you have the time and know-how.

From this information you form an opinion about what shares you want to buy and how many. But when do you buy them? Right, like everyone else, you want to buy low and sell high. You can rely on the professional analysts and see what they recommend as a price target; try to buy below that if they have a "buy" call on the stock. Or study the latest one-year chart of the stock and try to "buy on the dip", as the jargon says or just as the stock is about to break out on the upside. This is called technical analysis; chartists look for repeated chart patterns to give them buy or sell signals; they look for the 50-day moving average price to break out across and above the longer-term trend (the 200-day moving average) – for them this would be a bullish signal to buy. If you don't feel you are capable of "timing the market", as this strategy is called, just buy in when you have sufficient funds to invest. Most stock markets tend to go up over a long time horizon, and even the professional fund managers are rarely capable of getting their timing consistently right.

Besides, the psychology of investing tends to work against you. Many surveys and studies of so-called behavioural economics confirm that. When things look really bad and markets crash, retail investors have a propensity to panic and sell out; when everything looks rosy and safe, and your neighbour in the lift tells you about all the money he just made on this stock, you are likely to feel secure and buy in as well. That kind of euphoria usually signals an asset bubble, so that is all wrong. In fact you should do the exact opposite: Buy in when the market is depressed and sell out a bit when it is historically high!

You cannot rely purely on your intuition to help you in finance. Most likely your gut instincts will lead you astray; you have to respect the numbers, the statistics and the probabilities. Quick, there are 23 people in a room; what are the chances of two of them sharing the same birthday? It is 50-50. If there are 75 people in the room, the incident of two sharing the same birthday is almost assured – the probability is 99.9%. Not very obvious, is it, unless you are really good at math; but it is true. Our brains tend to work in a linear manner, when in fact numbers and economics work exponentially. So to conclude with one of those clichés that abound in the financial world: It is not your timing in the market that is important, it is your time in the market!

To execute the trade, you can set a low bid price target on your trading account and hope that a seller will turn up and bite. Say the offer price is $10 and there is a bid price of $9.80, but you only want to pay $9.50, then that is what you key in, and you wait – a day, a week or maybe a month. Alternatively, use the "To market" function and just buy at the available offer (or ask) price – in this case $10 – that the nearest seller is willing to unload at; you would do that if you want to catch a rising stock before it runs away from you.

A bit about stocks

Very basically, there are three types of companies that you look for, depending on your investment strategy. First, you have value stocks, where you try to identify valuable blue-chip companies selling at a market discount. Second are income stocks; these pay large dividends to shareholders. The dividend yield is easy to find on the internet; if it is 3–5% p.a., that would be considered good, beating current inflation and the rate you get on risk-free fixed income. Keep in mind that this dividend yield will not be attractive if the company cannot sustain it. The ratio – total yearly dividend payouts over share price – might be temporarily high because the denominator is low, and that denominator – the share price – could be low for a reason. Maybe the other investors know something that you don't. It could be that the company is crashing and will go even lower in the near future! Keep that in mind. Finally, there are the growth stocks. I mentioned Amazon before, but there are many others, particularly in the technology space. Usually these are smaller start-ups that may not even pay an annual dividend, but you might buy them if you think that capital gain – via the growth of the company and a higher share price – will generate an attractive overall return on your capital.

Stock-picking is a popular sport. There are many participants, and they usually all want to get rich quick. The good news is that in this game we can all be winners; there don't have to be any losers. When a rising tide lifts all boats, we will all do well; and for the last decade or so the tide has been rising quite nicely in most countries.

But will the tide always rise? Will the stock markets always go up? Of course not! At the moment, valuations seem stretched; overall PE ratios are high by historical standards. That has prompted investors like Marc Faber and Jeremy Grantham with generally bearish views to warn of a market crash, or at least a market correction of up to 40%. But then again, Grantham went on record last year (2017) to say that he has had to modify his sceptical outlook; in an interview he conceded that "this time it is decently different".[86] Meaning that we should get used to permanently higher asset prices, higher stock valuations and higher PE ratios overall as the new normal. Grantham could be right, or this could be a case of famous last words....

In the meantime, personally I have found that in general it is better to be in the market than out. If you have a portfolio of quality shares – and you try to protect the portfolio with some fixed income securities and precious metals for diversification – you are better off in the long run. If on top of that you own your home (and I mean *you* should own it, not the bank!), you don't really care if asset prices move up and out of whack. You are pretty safe that way, and if you enjoy some capital gain you just say "Thank you very much". Should the market crash – which it is likely to do one day – you merely ride it out, take it on the chin, as Grantham says. In a recession everyone is worse off, of course, but you are a little less worse off than others, because your quality portfolio will go down less than the overall market. Those who get badly hurt in a downturn and deflationary period are the poor, who have no financial reserves to cushion the fall if they lose their jobs and/ or get kicked out of their homes because they cannot service the mortgage; so don't be among those!

Today few people remember Tom Lehrer, I imagine, although he is still around as I write. When I was growing up, Lehrer was a mathematics professor with Harvard University; but he was also much more than that. Lehrer played the piano and sang, and during the 1960s he issued a wonderful selection of witty songs with a venomous satirical twist. I loved them then, and I wish I still had those old LP records today. Find the songs on YouTube if you can; you will not regret it. Lehrer's black humour has stood the test of time. One of his songs was "We will all go together when we go". The song was written in reference to the nuclear World War III, which never happened, of course, but which loomed large over us in the 60s. You could apply that thought to investing too: If there is a market slump, it is not so bad because we will all go (down) together for a while. Only those with no resources whatsoever or with debt will crash and burn completely.

Also, as an ethical investor you are even further protected. Remember the oil price collapse in 2014/2015? If you were heavily invested in fossil fuel stocks at the time, you would have gotten badly hit. In Singapore, blue-chip stock Keppel Corp dropped from S$11 per share to below S$5; SembMarine dropped from S$4.60 to S$1.30 during that period. Many smaller marine service companies fared even worse, and some got wiped out. Ezra Holdings, for one, could not service their bonds and had to go into default; they went down under a pile of debt and filed for bankruptcy in 2017. The shareholders lost everything.

For years, the AR-15 has been the weapon of choice for mass murderers in the US. It is a .223-calibre semi-automatic rifle that uses the deadly 5.56/45mm cartridge. It was developed by Colt, but Remington took up production and became associated with the model, calling it the Bushmaster. When the American public in 2017–2018 finally had enough of school shootings and other violent assaults involving the AR-15, Remington's business went south very quickly, and the company filed for bankruptcy.[87] The management approached some 30 different lenders, but not a single one wanted to give them any more capital. Remington is one of America's oldest and largest manufacturers of firearms, but they had to surrender to the power of the political consumer and investor. Both groups were simply fed up; they abandoned the company and brought it to its knees. In the process, the unethical investors lost all their money.

Not that ethical shareholders cannot also get burnt – we will look at that in the next chapter – but broadly speaking, it pays for investors to keep an eye on the public sentiment out there. When the sentiment shifts, it can shift pretty quickly, and then it is important to stay on the right side of the trade.

Before we move on from the single-company issue, please note that there are some companies that you cannot buy into. The Lego Group is one such company. It is owned by the Christiansen family and it is not for sale; the company never went public and is not listed on any stock exchange. Neither is IKEA, the world's largest furniture maker. This corporation is owned by a private foundation based in the Netherlands, which until 2018 was controlled by the Swedish founder; on paper the company is a charity, but it is run for profit and its status cleverly protects it from paying a lot more in corporate taxes and from hostile takeover bids by competitors. Privately owned companies are nimble, and in IKEA's case it has been able to make radical decisions such as setting up in Russia despite sanctions and taking drastic steps to go green and participating in the circular economy which we covered in Chapter 3. Something like this might not have been approved by shareholders, but private equity companies do not have to worry about that. The only thing is: they are also not so relevant to you – the investor – since you cannot invest in them!

Ethical funds

Maybe picking stocks individually is too much for you. It is time-consuming; first you have to study how to do it, then you have to do the fundamental analysis of multiple companies, and then you have to keep a constant eye on your holdings and tweak your portfolio regularly as economic conditions change. There is also an element of risk. If you get it wrong you might lose all your capital.

Enter the fund manager; he will do all this for you – for a fee. Mutual funds are actively managed and consist of a basket of assets selected and controlled by a capital management firm and its team of analysts and traders. ETFs – exchange-traded funds – are considered passive management; this type of fund will mimic and track an underlying group of assets such as a stock index; therefore ETFs are cheaper for the management company to handle and fees are lower.

It is important that you check the bid/offer spread that the fund offers; for mutual funds it can be as high as 2%. That means that should you buy into a fund and sell again the next day, you will have lost 4% of your capital right there! For ETFs the spread can be much smaller, as low as 0.05% for some products. I will not make any specific recommendations here; each service provider will announce their own terms and conditions and you will just have to find the product that is right for you. While you are at it, also check the so-called expense ratio, i.e. total yearly expenses over equity. It could be as high as 1.5% p.a. for some actively managed mutual funds; this is the amount that will come out of any dividends or capital gains you might make from the fund. Also make sure you check the expected yield, i.e. the yearly dividends from holdings that the fund will pass on to investors over the current price. Past yields are no guarantee of future performance, of course, but they will give you some idea of what to expect.

ETFs are not only cheaper to buy and sell and hold, they are also more liquid. As their implies, ETFs are traded on a stock exchange, and as such you can buy and sell at any time of the day while the exchange is open for business. In contrast, the price of a mutual fund is calculated at the end of each day using the NAV – net asset value – over number of units in the fund, and that is the price you will pay when you buy it the next day, usually through a bank or another financial institution. So with ETFs being so cheap and easy to trade, passive management is obviously the growing trend among investors and capital management companies at the moment. I find this ETF tracker useful: etfdb.com. The information you get is astonishing, and you can spend hours just researching all the wonderful possibilities there for putting you money to work. By buying into a basket of stocks, you spread your risk and benefit, in principle, from experts composing and managing these financial products. Upside potential might be somewhat limited, but so is the downside risk compared to owning one or just a few volatile companies.

But we are ethical investors, right? So let us narrow down the search a bit to ethical/SRI products. In *Green Money*, Sarah Pennells presents a selection of ethical mutual funds that you might want to consider, even if her selection is a bit UK-centric. But then, the UK has a tradition of nature appreciation: The local birdwatching club (RSPB) has some one million members, while the broader-based conservation society (the National Trust) has over four million! Imagine if the Nature Society in Singapore had a proportionate 340,000 members – that would be something, wouldn't it? (We have 1,500.)

Back to the UK, they are indeed a hub for ethical investing, as you could have guessed; they even have an Ethical Investment Association (EIA), an Ethical Property Company and a host of ethical retail banks with ethical savings accounts and ethical mortgages. Also check out the EIRIS Foundation, yourethicalmoney.org and, not least, blueandgreentomorrow.com. That last outfit publishes

Some profitable ethical funds

The following list by no means indicates an endorsement on my part; the final choice is entirely your own. However, the list is from the American financial research firm Morningstar Inc and goes to show that some ethical mutual funds do alright. The list might give you some idea about what to look for when you evaluate an ethical fund: its inclusion/exclusion policy, size, costs and past performance. Check the similar parameters of the funds you might be considering before you invest. Preferably dig into the fund further and see exactly what companies are included and with what weightage.

In this case, please keep in mind that these funds are all listed on the tech-heavy NASDAQ in the US, and that this index as a whole went up by some 25% from June 2016 to July 2017 and 11.6% compounded three years prior to that. Most of these ethical funds did quite well over one year, but only one actually beat the benchmark over three years.

Name	Size (US$ mil)	Expense ratio (%)	Jun 2016 – Jul 2017 return (%)	3-year compounded return (%)	Policy
Fidelity Select Environmental and Alternative Energy Portfolio	175	0.94	31.3	7.9	Invests in renewable energy and environmental services
Parnassus Endeavor Investor	4,380	0.95	31	14.5	Screens out fossil fuels; screens in good ESG practices
Eventide Gilead N	1,370	1.43	28.3	7	Screens out alcohol, guns, gambling, pornography; screens in good ESG practices
Calvert Emerging Markets Equity	312	0.92	28	5.1	Invests in emerging market companies with good ESG records involved in environmental services, health and poverty alleviation
Calvert International Opportunities Fund	190	1.16	27.5	4.2	Uses SRI and ESG principles to identify target companies

lots of ethical economic and social news as well as an excellent guide to sustainable investing in PDF format. This guide has a chart of the major green and ethical funds available, and there are a lot of them! In a user-friendly manner, each fund ticks off in the chart which type of companies they either screen out or aim to include, pretty much according to our list of values in the last chapter.

Most of these ethical funds based in the US, Europe or elsewhere can probably be accessed from Singapore, or wherever you are. If your bank or online platform don't have them, ask for them to be included; it is quite likely that the management will add them in. Alternatively you can buy in online, directly from the issuer. Singapore is of course a major wealth management centre in its own right; but with regard to ethics, just not so much; this is a market that is still in its infancy in Asia. But do talk to your local bank and ask them what they offer in terms of ethical investing products. Then don't take your bank officer's word for it; go online yourself and check what the recommended product actually consists of. With much fanfare, the Swiss private bank UBS launched what they called "the first pure green investment portfolio in Asia" in 2018.[88] But if you read the small print, the portfolio is only available to wealthy investors; the minimum input is US$500,000. The portfolio consists of 54% in stocks, 5% in cash or cash equivalents and 41% in green bonds.

Green bonds? Yes, surprise, surprise, of course there is such a thing as green bonds. But before you buy them, check how green they actually are. Green bonds are supposed to finance renewable energy projects and such, but only 10% of green bonds from China sold in 2016 had independent verification on the use of proceeds; some were used to construct so-called "clean coal" power stations.[89] During a conference in Singapore in 2018, the Lebanese-British financier Assaad Razzouk said: "I've looked at green bond issuers over the last two years, and the list of issuers is a joke.

Some 90% of green bonds appear to have been issued as transactions to save yield, look good, or greenwash, with no actual impact on the ground."[90] Maybe you'd better stick to the ethical equity funds.

So, to summarise: By selecting an ethical mutual fund or ETF of your choice, you avoid the risk and the time involved in picking and managing a portfolio of individual stocks. You establish an outlook for what you think the future might bring, and then you select a fund that matches your values at the lowest cost.

Personally I prefer to pick individual stocks. That is a hobby of mine and I have the time and the training to do this with a level of confidence. I don't always get it right, but often I do, and that is part of the thrill of investing. Bonds, however, are different; I keep some fixed income products in my portfolio to balance my exposure, and those I keep in mutual funds. It is a bit expensive (I typically pay about 1.2% per annum in expense ratio), but I prefer active management in this space, as there is a significant danger to international high-yield corporate bonds – as well as emerging market sovereign debt – both regarding currency fluctuations and default risk. Regarding precious metals, I keep a bit of gold as a hedge, around 3–5% of my net worth. Here I don't use ETFs; I buy and store (safely) the actual physical metal. In fact, personally I don't use ETFs that much myself, although I recommend them to others!

Institutional ethics

In SRI investment discussions, the issue of engagement usually comes up. As an ethical investor there are several ways you can influence events. One – as we have covered – is to actively screen your portfolio, negatively for garbage companies and positively for those you like. Another way is to engage with the company you own. If you are a registered shareholder, you are invited to annual general meetings in the corporation and you are allowed to speak on those occasions. Ask questions and make your voice heard; you can even put forward proposals. My son owns some shares in Statoil, the Norwegian government-linked oil company, now renamed Equinor. I bought them for him shortly after he was born as a long-term investment, and we still hold on to them; other than that I don't invest in fossil fuels anymore. Every year we get an invitation to the Statoil AGM, and every year some activist shareholders will put forward proposals such as: Statoil should stop drilling in the Arctic. Statoil should get out of the nasty Canadian tar sands fields. One proposal even called for Statoil to get out of the fossil fuel business altogether and convert 100% to renewables! Every year these proposals are all voted down by the majority shareholders, but the next year the activists are back trying their luck. At least they manage to make a point that way.

If you own 100 shares in DBS Bank and you turn up at the AGM and complain that the management is lending money to palm oil producers who clear the rainforest and burn what is left, Piyush Gupta is unlikely to pay much notice. If Temasek Holdings did that, he might pay attention; the Singapore government directly owns more than 11% of the company – some 284,145,301 shares the last time I checked.[91] This way, major shareholders can exert their influence, and many ethical investors do.

But then, Temasek doesn't claim to be an ethical investor. Temasek Holdings Pte Ltd is an investment company wholly owned by the Singapore government and regarded as a national wealth fund. The senior management travel to the usual sustainable business conferences and always repeat the mantra that growth is necessary and that you can care for the environment and grow the economy in harmony. GIC – the Government of Singapore Investment Corporation – is the second of the main pillars in the management of public financial reserves in Singapore; this company is a sovereign wealth fund and invests the country's public savings and pension funds, mainly in a portfolio of assets held abroad. The main goal of GIC is to protect and grow the savings of Singapore; yield is the prime concern. Regarding ethics, the company has issued this fairly broad and general statement (taken from its website): "As a long-term investor, we believe companies with good sustainability practices are more likely to perform better over time. We integrate sustainability considerations holistically into our investment process, as well as corporate practices and procurement process."[92] GIC's core values include prudence, respect, integrity, merit and excellence – things I believe we can all agree on. But to my knowledge, no detailed ethical policy or screening procedures have been announced.

The Government Pension Fund Global of Norway – popularly called the Oil Fund – has one of those: a detailed ethical policy. It is set out in four pages of guidelines and revised yearly by a five-member committee, the Council on Ethics, appointed by the Ministry of Finance.[93] The guidelines cover both fixed income and equity investments by the fund and aim to exclude from the portfolio companies that produce tobacco, weapons that "violate fundamental humanitarian principles" and coal (for more than 30% of revenue), as well as companies that violate human rights, cause severe environmental damage or use corrupt practices.

The long list of companies that the Oil Fund does not invest in (both shares and corporate debt) is available online.[94] The list is updated regularly and is in essence a who's-who of nasty corporate predators. It is interesting reading, but I will not go into all the details here. Let me just point out a few well-known corporations that spring to mind: How about Boeing? Don't they make those wonderfully comfortable airplanes we all fly in? Yes, but they also make horrible rockets for nuclear bombs, and the European Airbus SE is not much better, so out they go. Walmart Inc, the largest retailer in the world, with 2.3 million employees – isn't that just a harmless bunch of big shops? The Norwegians don't think so; they accuse the company of violating human rights and labour rights, and they do not invest. Rio Tinto Ltd, Barrick Gold Corp, Freeport McMoRan Copper and Gold Inc? Dirty mining. And locally, Genting Bhd – severe environmental damage. The question now is: Where do you even stop? Is there in reality a mining company or a palm oil producer out there that does not cause "severe environmental damage"? The good Norwegians in the Council of Ethics have their work cut out for them.

And now to the question on everyone's lips regarding ethics: Can you be ethical and still make money? The Norwegians answer this question with unequivocal clarity: YES, YOU CAN! The Norwegian pension fund at over a trillion dollars is the largest in the world. It has surpassed the public savings of China, Saudi Arabia, Qatar, Singapore and all the other wealthy nations in the world. The country has 5.3 million people. Don't ever tell me that you cannot be ethical and make a buck at the same time. In fact, I think that not only will you be happier if you do the right thing, you will also be richer over the long haul.

Value of Norway's Oil Fund
(billions of kroners, at 30/07/17 prices)

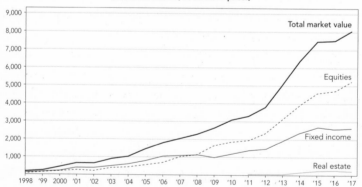

This chart shows the value of the Norwegian government's Pension Fund Global, the so-called Oil Fund, over the last 20 years. Strict ethical guidelines are applied, and still the public nest egg is doing quite nicely.

In the next two chapters we will look at how you can apply your positive screening preferences and consider the opportunities for some specific profitable ethical investments.

7

Energetic Investing

"The greenest car is one that does not exist."
— LAND TRANSPORT AUTHORITY
(SINGAPORE)

Fossil fuels are old sunshine

Do you remember the 10 ethical themes that Janus Henderson Investors identified for positive screening (Chapter 5; see page 88)? Let us look at them in a bit more detail. In this chapter I will cover ethical energy and transport – the largest and most important of the themes, economically and socially. Then in the next chapter, I will look at all the other themes together and explore their potential for ethical investors.

The world was a very different place 150–200 million years ago. Instead of a 3,000-metre-thick ice cap, there were dense forests on the South Pole, and dinosaurs roamed there, even during the dark winter months. Of course, the earth had the same slant on its axis facing the sun, it rotated the same way, the days had the same length as they have now during the various seasons. What was different were the position of the continents, and the level of carbon dioxide in the atmosphere – it was four to five times higher than it is now, and the world was simply a much warmer place in general.[95] In that period and over the next millions of years, there was an enormous die-off of oceanic zooplankton and algae which collected on the sea bed. Trapped inside porous sediment mud and sealed off from above by an impermeable rock cap, the material was starved of oxygen; under pressure and high temperatures it turned into hydrocarbons, i.e. oil and gas. Coal formed even earlier – some 300 million years ago – from compressed plant matter. As so much carbon got trapped underground, the CO_2 level in the atmosphere gradually decreased, and the climate cooled down, allowing sea levels to drop.

Photosynthesis generated the old carbon deposits in the first place, so in essence, fossil fuels are old sunshine that has been stored underground for millions of years. When we dig this material out – or suck it up with a jack-pump – we are in reality digging up old bones and excavating extra energy. When we burn the hydrocarbons off in a combustion process, we are releasing the carbon – old ghosts that were stored safely down there to good effect – thousands of gigatons of it every year. Discharged again, the carbon atoms combine in molecules – in the form of CO_2, methane and other gases – that are now causing a new die-off of life on Earth. The main difference is the time scale: While the storage happened over millions of years, the release has happened in just the last few centuries, which by evolutionary standards is just the blink of an eye. People alive now are likely to experience atmospheric CO_2 at twice today's level, and as a consequence they might see the day when Amsterdam, Jakarta, Bangkok and New York will have to be evacuated because of rising sea levels.

It is no wonder that people in general have a hard time getting their heads around this. It is tempting to go into denial. Of course everyone can see that the global air and sea temperatures are rising – no one can deny that. But it is fairly easy to convince yourself that this is caused by temporary solar activity; it is just a cycle, we can do nothing about it, surely the climate will go back to normal and get cooler again soon. In her book *This Changes Everything*, Naomi Klein documents that in Alberta, Canada – a region heavily dependent on the fossil fuel economy – only 41% of residents told pollsters during a survey that humans are contributing to climate change. Surveys in Appalachian coal country and along the Gulf Coast in the US show similar results; while in Atlantic Canada – far from the oil fields – 68% of respondents said that humans are warming the planet. That doesn't mean that people in Alberta are dumber than other Canadians; it just means that, as Klein concludes, "the bottom line is that we are all inclined to denial when the truth is too costly". In *Bad Science* (2008), Ben Goldacre writes about this phenomenon: "'Communal reinforcement' is the process by which a claim becomes a strong belief, through repeated assertion by members of a community." This happens all the time, especially regarding environmental issues in general, and global warming in particular.

Everywhere you go, people are burning off stuff and turning the landscape into agriculture, urban sprawl and industrial wastelands. It is common sense that tampering with nature on this colossal scale will have some consequences. But first of all, sometimes it looks as if common sense is not that common after all, but in fact quite a rare commodity. And secondly, even if you accept a link between fossil fuel consumption and climate change, what can you do about it? Companies typically have a quarter-year time horizon; if they don't show a growing bottom line with each quarterly report, the market will hammer their stock price down mercilessly. The stock price matters to companies: a higher price will improve investors' confidence, so the company can borrow at a lower cost and ensure smooth operations; staff also feel more confident, and so the best people can be retained. Politicians' time horizon might be a bit longer, at least till the next election cycle, which is usually four or five years down the road. Ordinary people have to make ends meet year to year; it seems to me far-fetched to ask them right now to give up driving and become vegetarians and have one child instead of three, just on the odd chance that their current habits may or may not cause some damage to future generations hundreds of years from now. It is a lot to ask, and in all honesty, that is unlikely to happen.

So what is about to happen at this point is that changes will soon be forced upon us. In his aptly named book *The Race for What's Left: The Global Scramble for the World's Last Resources* (2012), Michael Klare writes: "As the race for what's left gains momentum, it will intrude with greater force into world affairs, threatening the survival of animal species, local communities, giant corporations, and entire nations. Only if we abandon the race altogether, focusing instead on developing renewable resources and maximising efficiency, can we hope to avoid calamity on a global scale." In other words, business as usual simply cannot continue without catastrophic consequences for those in the firing line, i.e. the poor and the poorly prepared. Their displacement, migration and resistance will upset everyone else as well. So since there is no indication currently that we will be able to change our ways, I say: Plan for trouble down the road and position yourself correctly!

We subsidise the burning

The fossil fuel companies and their financiers are not going to give up so easily; they have billions of dollars at their disposal to advertise and promote their points of view. In his excellent book *The Subsidy Scandal: How Your Government Wastes Your Money To Wreck Your Environment* (2002), Charlie Pye-Smith exposes the lobbying that goes on, not just from fossil fuel companies but also from industries involved in forestry, agriculture, fishing, water supply and construction. Together these industries receive yearly US government subsidies in excess of $700 billion, subsidies that Pye-Smith calls perverse: "Subsidies that are bad both for the economy and for the environment." Quoting a US government report, Pye-Smith identifies "a dizzying array of subsidies, ranging from price support to tax exemptions and low-cost loans, from exemptions from environmental laws to the provision of cheap services and import tariffs". The book is somewhat US-centric and already 16 years old, yet I am sure a similar case – or an even stronger one – could be made today for most countries in the world. As an example, Pye-Smith writes: "Worldwide, subsidies to the automobile probably exceed forest subsidies by a factor of ten." That's another reason why I like to be based in Singapore, where the official policy is explicitly to move towards a "car-lite" future.

Take Europe; yes, European countries tax petrol and diesel to varying degrees, but in countries like France and especially Germany, the government has a very cosy relationship with the car industry, something that came to light during the diesel car emissions scandal in 2015.[96] Briefly, secret software was installed in diesel cars to make emissions appear lower – by as much as 40 times. This way the cars could qualify for "clean fuel" tax breaks and enjoy better overall sales. That scandal broke because American – not German – authorities uncovered massive criminal fraud practices, not just in Volkswagen but among all the other major German car makers as well, starting with a secret agreement to cheat as early as the 1990s.[97] *Fortune* magazine called the Volkswagen diesel cheating scandal "one of the most audacious corporate frauds in history". In spite of this, while penalties were dished out in America, Fortune.com writes in 2018: "In Germany, where the key decisions were made and all the decision makers reside, no criminal or administrative fines or penalties have yet been imposed.... In Europe, where the company sold 8 million tainted diesels, VW has not paid a single Euro in government penalties."[98] Keep in mind that in Europe alone, where 72,000 people die too early each year because of deadly nitrogen oxides in the air, 7,000 of those deaths can be directly linked to exhaust from diesel vehicles.[99] That is many more than the number who die from terrorist-related activities in Europe: 61 in 2017.

I cannot go into too much detail here, but let me quickly bring up the Common Agricultural Policy within the EU. More than anything else, it is well documented that this disastrous policy has for decades wreaked havoc on the European environment. The policy has provided billions of Euros of subsidies to farmers every year since its implementation in 1962; in this way it has promoted the production of unhealthy products like sugar, meat and yes, even tobacco. The policy has encouraged massive over-production; the landscape throughout Europe has been devastated by intensive farming, while high external tariffs have made it near impossible for farmers in Africa and South America to compete and gain entry into the European market. We are wrecking the environment, not just on borrowed funds and borrowed time, but with the help of Western governments and at the expense of taxpayers as well.

Can coal be clean? Can gas?

The latest catchphrase put out there by the fossil fuel lobby is "clean coal". If you ever saw a contradiction in terms, that is it. Briefly it involves cleaning the coal at source – at or near the mine – to remove impurities and excess water. This makes the raw material cheaper to transport and easier to burn. During combustion, better smokestacks are designed to reduce emission of harmful gases – apart from CO_2, of course – such as sulphur dioxide and nitrogen oxides.

Part of the clean coal campaign has been to introduce so-called "carbon capture and storage" (CCS). Isolating carbon and somehow reinjecting it into the ground of course makes no sense at all; it is costly and cumbersome and energy-intensive. Pilot studies have been done at great expense by Germans, Norwegians and others with money to burn, but this procedure has never worked on any significant scale and most likely never will. The flagship Norwegian CCS project at Mongstad was at one time hailed by then-PM Jens Stoltenberg as "Norway's moon landing". Then in 2011, the operator Aker Solutions pulled the plug on the idea, having wasted some $15 million already. "The (CCS) market is dead," its CEO told the press back then.[100] So it is back to the drawing board for the "clean coal" lobbyists.

But natural gas is alright, right? No, sorry. Natural gas is just another source of global warming; it may or may not be dirtier than coal, but it is never clean. Don't take my word for it; the US Environmental Protection Agency (EPA) for years underestimated the air pollution from natural gas. Natural gas does tend to burn cleaner, with less particle emissions and less CO_2 than refined crude oil and a lot less than coal. However, in 2014 the EPA concluded that the emission of methane from natural gas – which as a greenhouse gas is 30 times more potent than CO_2 – had been underestimated for years.[101] The gas leaks occur during production and transport and had not been accounted for properly. When gas is transported, it is either run through pipelines or cooled down as LNG – liquefied natural gas – and shipped on specially designed vessels. LNG is mainly methane (CH_4) cooled to below the dew point (-161°C), which also reduces its volume by some 600 times. This should not be confused with LPG – liquefied petroleum gas – which is mainly propane (C_3H_8) derived from petroleum refining and stored in pressurised tanks and containers. In Singapore, for instance, where natural gas is used in more than 90% of our electricity generation, we get a combination of natural gas piped directly from nearby gas fields in Malaysia and Indonesia, and as LNG, which can in theory be shipped from anywhere in the world. Although the piped-in gas is still most important – 77% of gas supplies – the LNG business is gaining ground.[102]

So the somewhat overlooked problem with natural gas in all its forms is that although it burns fairly cleanly, the leakage throughout the extraction and supply chain causes great harm to the environment. Something in the order of 1–3% of the gas leaks into the atmosphere before it can even be put to use. Under the headline "A dirty little secret", *The Economist* covered the issue of methane pollution from natural gas in 2016.[103] And many other experts and observers have taken this argument one step further and declared that natural gas might indeed be a dirtier fuel than coal. On lifescience.com you can read this conclusion: "Problematically, natural gas is prone to leaking from pipelines, wellheads, and the nooks and crannies of processing and storage facilities. 'Accounting for methane leakage throughout the supply chain of natural gas, natural gas might actually be worse for the climate than coal,' said Lena Moffitt, director of the Sierra Club's Stop Dirty Fuels Campaign."

All electric by 2025?

So our big shift to electric transport makes little sense as long as our electricity is generated mostly from oil, coal or yes, even natural gas. Personally I would love to see more electric cars on our streets. It does shift the pollution away from the roads at nose-level and back into a power plant somewhere out of town. That is nice in itself; but it is not going to save the planet. Overall – from drawing board to scrapyard – the typical electric automobile will pollute more than one with a small conventional combustion engine. Many surveys confirm that, and I quote some of them in *Be Financially Free*. As we have seen before, EVs only sell if they are subsidised, so the taxpayer loses out as well. Of the technologies available today, the gas- or diesel-electric hybrid vehicle makes the most sense. I honestly don't know why we don't have diesel-electric hybrid buses in Singapore – they have been available for decades – but I presume they cost a few dollars more to buy, and consumers are unlikely to take kindly to a 10-cent increase in fares.

Electric cars are great for the car industry; it is always excellent for manufacturing when we have to change everything out and dump the old stuff in a heap somewhere. There are people who have made it their life's mission to preach "disruption", such as Stanford University's Tony Seba, who is on record as saying that "by 2025 every new vehicle will be electric". Seba travels around the world to all the usual renewable energy conferences preaching that disruption is coming; in an interview in 2018 he said that people who dismiss the disruption gurus are "linear, siloed and backwards-looking".[104] I for one will admit to being fairly siloed, whatever that means.

I don't travel so much these days, but I was up in southern Thailand last year in December 2017 and had to fly home out of Bangkok. The drive up north took a few hours; it was another two hours to get across town to the airport through bumper-to-bumper 10-lane traffic moving at bicycle pace. There were lots of vehicles there for sure, but I don't recall seeing any electric cars. But in seven years only electric vehicles will be sold, according to Seba? How are they all going to be charged? What about the trucks and the tractors and the diesel-powered construction equipment – will they also be electric? It will be interesting to see how the Thais manage to pull that off.

As it turned out, I also visited Norway not too long after that, in May 2018. Yes, there you see plenty of brand new EVs on the road, generously subsidised by the state. Electric charging stations at all shopping malls as well. By market share, Norway has more electric cars on the road than any other country, and it even plans to have electric-only domestic air travel by 2040.[105] Across the border in Sweden, I was told that they are laying out roads with electric charging cables built into the tarmac, so the EVs charge as they go. Seba would love it there. It just seems to me that the world is breaking into two halves: The richest countries are staying afloat fairly nicely, the rest are sinking fast.

Back in Singapore, some 2% of the cars on the road are currently electric or hybrid electric – mainly hybrids and then mostly Toyota Prius taxis bought in previous years because of a generous government rebate scheme for hybrid cars that was discontinued in 2018. I like the first line on the LTA (Land Transport Authority) website about promoting clean and energy-efficient cars; it says: "The greenest car is one that does not exist."[106] I couldn't have put it better myself!

Disruption is coming, we are told; we will all switch to completely electric transport. Maybe, but even if we did, what about the source of the power? Currently, 2% of Singapore's power comes from renewable sources, mainly photovoltaic solar panels. According to the Economic Strategies Committee, a target has been set to increase this to 5% of Singapore's peak electricity demand or 350 MWp by 2020.[107] That will require rolling out solar panels on rooftops and floating on reservoirs. But that will most likely be as far as we can go; wind and nuclear power have basically been ruled out. Power-generating windows in buildings are still at the experimental stage. Most likely we will burn fossil fuels for 90% of our power consumption for as long as we can get it.

And the old system is doing just great, thank you. According to a 2018 survey conducted by Phillips, there is a flat-line in demand for power and excess supply; the article concludes: "The reserve margin in Singapore is around 90% (i.e. capacity installed is almost double peak demand), far above the minimum 30%. The take-or-pay LNG gas contracts exacerbate the supply situation."[108] The profit margins in the energy business are already razor-thin; the Hyflux Tuaspring 411 MW power plant has never made any money. Power generation in Singapore is a very competent business with high efficiency and great terms for consumers. So if it ain't broke, why fix it? The fact that the earth is dying does not really factor into that equation.

The solar options
Where does all that leave investors? It basically leaves us in a difficult spot. There is a tug-of-war going on at the moment, between renewable energy forces on one side and the old fossil fuel business on the other. We know we should switch to renewable energy, for

the sake of our health and to avoid further environmental damage to our ecosystem. But the old market forces are not giving up; they pull away hard on their end of the rope. Not counting the negative externalities – and as we saw in Chapter 3, we don't really have a mechanism for pricing them in – fossil fuels still appear to be the cheapest and most convenient energy source we have.

In the renewable energy corner we have all the do-gooders and the disruption gurus promoting a cleaner way forward. In the fossil fuel corner sit the old-school industry giants and their pro-growth cheerleaders, helped along nicely by public demand for cheap stuff at all cost and – as we have seen above – sympathetic governments as well. What investors can do is to try and ana-lyse the situation, foresee events and position themselves going forward. The economic shift towards renewables is undeniable. It might take a bit longer than some hopeful souls would like, it might not even be as definitive and complete, but the transforma-tion is undeniable.

What are the options for renewable energy sources? Where will the capital go? Where can you put yours to work and make a buck?

First of all, there is the solar power option. Solar basically comes in two technical forms: solar photovoltaic (PV); and solar thermal technology, the so-called power tower. PV technology con-verts solar rays into electricity using those solar panels we are all familiar with; they are an assembly of silicon-based semiconductor cells and can be installed anywhere on poles, rooftops or on an industrial scale across large fields. The power tower technology is an array of mirrors that concentrate the sun's rays onto a tower, where water is heated to generate steam and run electric turbines. The thermal-electric version is suitable mainly for industrial installations to provide power into the main grid; but the technol-ogy can also be scaled down to single-household or neighbourhood plants and be used directly to provide heating and hot water.

Solar power has to be our way forward – one way or another. Indeed, solar energy is the darling of all the green investment options out there. Yet, it has not been an easy ride so far for people investing in solar options. Like so many others, I personally got carried away during the solar investment craze in the late 2000s. The solar company Renewable Energy Corporation – later called REC – was one such investment favourite. Founded in Norway in 1996, it became one of the largest companies on the Norwegian stock exchange. It expanded into Europe, America and the Pacific, setting up operational headquarters in Singapore. In 2008, the company's stock price took a beating and dropped from NOK185 in November 2007 to around NOK40 in January 2009. I started buying some stocks during that period as I felt the market was oversold and cheap; and yes, I also bought into REC. A well-managed company based in two countries of my choice, doing good things, all at a beat-down price – what was there not to like?

Luckily, since I didn't know that much about the business and didn't have time in those days to do a full analysis of the company and its outlook, I just went in with a symbolic amount of NOK25,000, about US$3,000 – my average purchase price was 24 kroners per share. It was a classic case of "Don't try to catch a falling knife"! The general stock market famously bottomed out on 9 March 2009, but not REC (see chart on next page). It kept on dropping, falling to NOK14 in 2010. After that the company got into all kinds of trouble; it never ever paid any dividends to shareholders. In 2013 it had to be broken into two and shareholders got transferred into what is now REC Silicon. The stock price today? The last time I checked, it was 1 Norwegian krone and 30 øre; I have lost 95% of my money!

So much for being a nice guy and investing green. I would have been ruined today if I had poured all my money into green stocks in those days. Luckily I didn't, and the bank shares I bought during that period have done pretty nicely, thank you! Now the

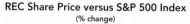

REC Share Price versus S&P 500 Index
(% change)

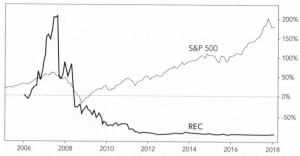

This chart shows the variations in share price of solar energy champion Renewable Energy Corporation (REC) from 2006 to May 2018; the baseline is 1998. For comparison is the S&P 500 index throughout the same period. Yes, buying stocks during the beginning of 2009 was a good idea, but not buying REC; that company has lost virtually all its value, while the overall market benchmark has gone up quite nicely.

advantage for you is that you can learn from my mistake and be more careful with your own investment decisions.

What happened? During the 2010s a deluge of cheap made-in-China solar systems flooded the world markets. The Chinese government spent $47 billion on tax breaks and incentives to the industry, and between 2008 and 2013 world prices of solar panels dropped by some 80%.[109] Manufacturers in Europe and America buckled under the competition and many went under completely. On greentechmedia.com you can find the long list of solar-related companies that went bankrupt or got bought up by others for next to nothing.[110]

And yet, for all that, overall the solar business has been growing. In the US, the solar industry generated $42 billion worth of business in 2007; in 2017 it was $154 billion. That year, some 25% of new power plant installations were solar. The industry directly or indirectly employs 370,000 people; compare that to the coal industry, which only supports 160,000 jobs. In Europe and China, the growth has been similar. The challenge for investors has mainly been to navigate through the bubble of over-capacity in solar installations and the falling prices. Yes, falling prices have been good for consumers, but not so good for return on capital.

So the demand for solar is growing and the industry is expanding; nevertheless, start-ups struggle to make money, with many going belly-up. Under such conditions investors would do well to spread their risk. Rather than pick individual companies, they should take advantage of products like mutual funds or ETFs to secure exposure to a basket of companies. Even if one or two go bust, the growth of the others will make up for it. That is also the thinking of individual VCs – or so-called angel investors – investing in unlisted early-stage start-ups with the potential for huge growth. A VC might pick 10 companies and invest; nine might go broke, but if just one makes it to an IPO and the share price goes up 20 times, he has still doubled his money!

The S&P 500 Global Clean Energy Index is a decent gauge of how the clean energy space has progressed lately. It offers exposure to 30 companies from around the world that are involved in clean-energy-related businesses (not just solar):

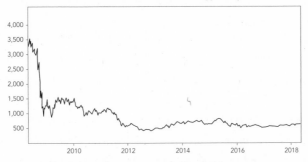

S&P 500 Global Clean Energy Index

The S&P 500 Global Clean Energy Index's performance over the past 10 years from May 2008 to May 2018. After the disastrous 2008–2009 period, the clean energy space is stabilising and recovering slowly.

I think you will find that if you select an ETF such as the iShares Global Clean Energy ETF, it will track this index fairly accurately; in fact, this particular ETF has outperformed its benchmark by a small margin. Using the iShares product, $10,000 invested in May 2013 would have grown by 30% to around $13,000 in May 2018, a quite respectable compounded return of 5.4% p.a. over five years. So do-gooders can make money after all. Only, as an ordinary retail investor you would do well to use a fund to spread your risk. And if you are an institutional investor, you have to put in a lot of research hours, and even then spread your eggs out among many baskets.

Blowing in the wind

In terms of sheer scale, the only other industry matching solar in the renewable energy space is wind power. To continue with the US as a case study, the wind turbine industry employs just over 100,000 people in that country, somewhat less than solar, and yet contributes around 6% of the electricity supply – for solar, in spite of all the hype, it is still only around 2%. Only China and the EU have more wind power capacity than the US; in China some 4% of electricity is generated from wind power.

The interesting thing about wind power is its rapid growth. The US Department of Energy is targeting 10% wind power generation by 2020; in Germany the percentage for 2017 was up to 20% from 16% just the previous year; in Denmark 44% of electricity was generated by wind power in 2017.[111] Sure, that swift increase has to a large extent been due to public subsidies. Although renewable energy hasn't quite enjoyed the subsidies that the fossil fuel industry has, various government assistance schemes in all countries have helped to make this type of electricity generation competitive. As the industry matures, these subsidies are expected to be scaled back, and the renewable energy industry will increasingly be expected to stand on its own two feet.

And it is not as if the wind industry is without controversy. Those who follow this topic will know that windmills are not always popular, thanks to the NIMBY syndrome – Not In My Back Yard! Everyone supports green energy – on paper, as long as it is installed somewhere else. Windmills are ugly, windmills make noise, windmills kill birds – that sort of thing. I will leave it to you, the reader, to sort through the chatter yourself. Personally I don't have a strong opinion about this. I would tweak the LTA statement and say: The greenest power plant is one that does not exist! But since we apparently must have some new power plants, wind turbines are the lesser of the evils available.

And I must say that I have been a bit luckier investing in wind power than in solar. I invest for two reasons: because I like windmills better than fossil fuels, and because I think I can make my money grow that way and become free, financially and otherwise. While anyone can assemble a few PV solar panels in his basement and set up a solar energy start-up service provider, it is not so easy with wind energy. You need a company of scale to produce, install and service a monstrous 9.5-megawatt wind turbine capable of powering some 8,000 homes on its own. Vestas Wind Systems A/S, listed on the Copenhagen stock exchange, can do that. As an investor, you look for a business segment where the entry level is fairly high – your money is safer from competition there – and the solar business is just not one of those. Besides, unlike solar, where the Chinese exporters killed off the solar panel market, those huge wind turbines are not easy to ship; most are manufactured quite close to the point of application. That reality provides further protection from cheap Asian competition within the large mature markets of Europe and the US.

Even then, the competition in the wind turbine business is fierce, and the prices are under pressure. That might be good for consumers, but it is not so good for investors. After Denmark's Vestas, the major wind turbine companies in order of market share

are Germany and Spain's recently combined Siemens Gamesa, GE, China's Goldwind, and Germany's Enercon; India's Suzlon ranks in 10th place. In March 2018, Bloomberg observed that all the major players in the industry had seen their share prices decline year-over-year; the piece had the encouraging title: "We All Love Wind Power, Unless You Want to Make Money."[112] This I don't agree with. I have done alright here, by buying low and selling high, and I still own shares in Vestas; it has been a great investment for me, and I love the company, volatile as it may be. In the meantime, some further consolidation might have to take place in the industry, and on top of that it is virtually impossible for individual investors – and even for professional analysts – to predict which company will get the fat contracts at the right price in the future and grow their bottom-line numbers; therefore you either have to spread your holdings across several of the promising players or find an ETF with heavy exposure to wind power, and indeed there are plenty of those.

What is certain is that wind power is here to stay. It is not going to go away anytime soon. I am convinced that there is potential in this space. Look at the chart below, which shows the global wind energy capacity in megawatts. I think it is safe to say that the bars will keep on growing for the foreseeable future, so capitalise on that.

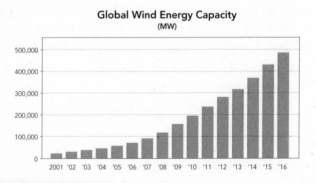

Global Wind Energy Capacity
(MW)

About the real Tesla

Let me highlight a few more alternatives to fossil fuels – some are economically significant, others are still in their experimental stage.

First, there is the good old hydroelectric dam. Tesla built the first one at the Niagara Falls between the US and Canada in 1895.[113] No, not Tesla Inc, the real Tesla: Nikola Tesla, who Elon Musk named his company after. Nikola Tesla was an amazing inventor and entrepreneur credited with the development of AC (alternating current) power, which revolutionised our use of power over a very short time span at the end of the 19th century and the beginning of the 20th. Hydropower had been used long before that, and even in pre-industrial times river flows were used to drive huge grinding wheels in watermills to crush grain and perform other mechanical tasks. It was the method of converting this rotating energy into electricity that was so revolutionary.

Do you know which country in Europe is big on hydroelectric energy? Right, Norway again – they just have everything going for them up there! Long before oil and gas were found in the North Sea, the Norwegians had been damming up their rivers to harness the power of falling water. Their tall, deep fjords and rocky, largely treeless foundation are perfect for this technology. So through their foresight and technology – and with a bit of luck from their geological arrangement – the Norwegians have had the good fortune of cheap, clean power. In Norway, one kWh (kilowatt hour) of electricity costs on average EUR0.15 including taxes; in nearby Denmark it is double, EUR0.30.[114] The cost in Singapore is similar to Norway's, but that is mainly because our taxes and general cost structure are lower, not because we use cheap and abundant and clean and sustainable energy to generate electricity, like the Viking descendants do.

So sometimes life is funny that way: The country that accumulated a $1 trillion nest egg from selling fossil fuels to others gets 98% of its own power from renewable energy. Which reminds me of an interview that was playing on television some time back with one of the Marlboro Man male models. Remember the Marlboro Man? While cigarette advertising was still allowed, he was the hunky cowboy riding his horse across the Western frontier while smoking. In the interview, this actor reminisced that during the Marlboro Man photo-shoot, executives from Philip Morris (owners of the Marlboro brand) would fly out to location by helicopter; they would camp there and spend the night, so that they could supervise that early morning sun-up scene with the crew. The actor would pass cigarettes around at the evening camp fire, but the executives would all decline and say: "We don't smoke that s***. We just sell it!" That documentary was filmed shortly before the handsome actor died of lung cancer.

While hydropower works well in remote mountainous terrain with barren rock, little tree cover and thin population density, it is not for everyone. There are many disadvantages associated with hydropower; too many dams along one river might impede water flow and wreak havoc on communities downstream. Along the Nile, the Mekong and the Yangtze, environmentally friendly dams have turned out to be not so friendly socially and politically. On the island of Borneo, the Bakun Dam in Sarawak, Malaysia, has been pretty much a technical, ecological and economical disaster; in view of that, the nearby Baram Dam was cancelled after protests from opponents.[115] Hydroelectric power simply doesn't work so well in populated, forested areas with loose topsoil, where people have to be displaced to form the dams, and the new lakes quickly fill up with silt washing down from the hills.

Geothermal and such

Like Norway, Iceland is an amazing Nordic country that is punching way above its weight class in the international boxing match. The country of 330,000 people made it to the quarter-finals of the

2016 UEFA European football championships, beating England in the process; they qualified top of their group for the 2018 FIFA World Cup, while countries like Italy and Netherlands didn't make it. There they were knocked out during the opening rounds, but they still managed a respectable draw against former world champions Argentina. With regard to energy, Iceland gets some 85% of its primary energy from a totally sustainable and clean source: geothermal. It has been pronounced the "greenest country in the world", as measured by the Environmental Sustainability Index operated by Guinness World Records.[116] Icelandic officials like to travel the world and proclaim that if we can do it, so can you.

That is of course a bit of a stretch. Not all countries are situated on top of a bunch of volcanoes and shallow reservoirs full of steaming-hot water. However, even on a smaller scale, power in the form of geothermal heat has a lot of potential. There are basically two methods of using the heat from the earth: directly, by installing a system of geothermal heat pumps to propel up warm water from below and circulate it to heat up houses, offices and agricultural plants; and indirectly, by drilling deeper to find hot water and steam to run electric power generators. Either system works well, in my opinion. This is proven and fairly simple technology that can be scaled down to single-household schemes (direct heat) or scaled up to run large industrial power systems. The countries that generate the most electricity from geothermal power are the US, Philippines, Indonesia, Mexico and Italy, in that order. And although the numbers in general are small, locally the impact can be significant. In the Philippines, geothermal accounts for some 13% of power generated; with hydropower, solar and wind thrown in, 25% of the Philippines' power generation is from renewable sources.[117] You can check the International Geothermal Association website for more information.[118] Suffice it to say that if you get the opportunity to invest in a green fund with a geothermal component, consider it; this is a field with a future.

I cannot, however, say that about most of the other alternative energy sources that are in the news now and then. Personally I don't like nuclear power; I don't think it is our solution for a carbon-lite destiny. I know a lot of people would disagree with me on that, so I will just leave it there. I just cannot see that nuclear power offers any worthwhile opportunities for capital allocation.

Nuclear reactors of course work on fission energy, i.e. the splitting of atoms. But there is also such a thing as fusion energy. This is the power used in thermonuclear weapons, or hydrogen bombs. If we could make peaceful use of fusion power, we would have it made. Imagine if we could make unlimited amounts of power by melting hydrogen – like the sun does – but in a controlled manner in a nuclear reactor. Well, don't hold your breath. It has been said about the fusion reactor that it is just 30 years away, but in spite of billions of dollars being poured into research over the years, it is still 30 years away, and it probably always will be.[119]

On the subject of hydrogen, this amazing element plays the central role in another application: fuel cell technology. In a fuel cell, H_2 is passed through a so-called proton exchange membrane. There the H_2 combines with oxygen – O_2 – to produce H_2O + heat + electricity. The electricity can power an electric motor that can drive a big fancy Mercedes car. Hey, finally we got this thing licked; we are always looking for ways where we can go on living and growing and wasting just like we always have, but without cost to the environment. Surely fuel cell technology is it – a car that runs miraculously on abundant hydrogen and with just a bit of water coming from the exhaust, right?

No, sorry, not so fast. To get the hydrogen in the first place, we have to use much more energy than we will ever produce running it through the fuel cell later! The numbers simply don't add up. But of course that hasn't stopped the various car companies like Toyota, General Motors and Daimler (i.e. Mercedes) from bringing out prototype fuel cell cars. But that is all they will ever be: prototypes. You can only speculate that the big car makers do this for promotional reasons; these vehicles will never be practical transport for the mass market. Even Elon Musk of Tesla Inc – who thrives on disruption and revolutionary new technology – has dismissed fuel cell transport as fantasy. He is on record as calling fuel cells "fool cells", "mind-bogglingly stupid" and "incredibly dumb".[120]

I will leave you to judge for yourself all the other brilliant ideas out there regarding renewable energy – wave power, tidal power, biological solar energy (making fuel from algae), etc. Get a copy of Armstrong & Blundell's excellent book *Energy... Beyond Oil* (2007); although 10 years old it is still a superb catalogue of all the options available, their technical details and practical pros and cons.

Investment ramifications

Before we move on from the SRI/ethical energy space, let us try to cut through some of the hype surrounding clean energy. Correct, we have to reduce our CO_2 and other GHG emissions. In this chart you can see where most of the CO_2 is coming from:

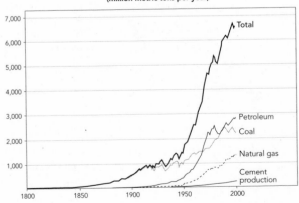

Oil, coal and natural gas are the three largest CO_2 sources.

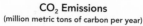

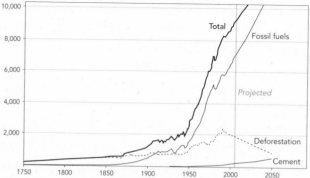

In this chart, deforestation is included as well, so the total carbon emissions are somewhat higher; furthermore, the emissions are expanded with estimated values to the middle of the century. Notice that our deforestation rate is not likely to continue, simply because we are running out of virgin forest to cut, especially in Southeast Asia and Africa (there is still some left in South America). But our use of fossil fuels keeps expanding!

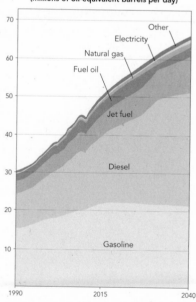

This graphic provides a breakdown of our power sources converted to a uniform measurement: oil-equivalent barrels per day. The projected data is provided by the oil business, and notice how they predict – correctly, in my opinion – that we will go on flying and driving pretty much like we always have, only more and more. What happened to Tony Seba's "all electric by 2025"? It doesn't seem to be on the cards.

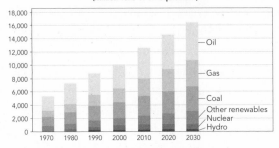

World Primary Energy Demand
(million tons of oil-equivalent)

And finally there is the primary energy demand for the whole world as projected to 2030 by the International Energy Agency. Seba and other disruption gurus don't think so highly of the mainstream IEA, but what if they are right?

The conclusion is that the rumours of the death of the oil business are somewhat exaggerated. The clean energy lobby might be right in saying that we should leave most of the fossil stuff deep underground where it belongs. If we do that, yes, then the huge energy reserves that hold up the share price of fossil fuel producers will become worthless, so-called stranded assets, and those lofty share prices will come crashing down. Alternatively, a future global recession triggered by a debt crisis – which in my view is quite likely – could also hit the oil business hard. Because of the very inelastic nature of the price and demand variables for an essential commodity like crude oil, a small drop in demand can cause – and on some occasions has caused – a disproportionate drop in price. So personally I avoid fossil fuel investments, but I can see why others would still want to pursue them for many decades to come. Even the managers of the ethical Norwegian Pension Fund do not avoid oil business investments – how could they, it is called the Oil Fund!

Have a look at the charts again and notice how small a percentage of our near-future power and transport needs are expected to be from clean energy; all in all very little. And another thing, when I meet the clean energy disruption proponents at events, I try to find out what the consequences of this conversion to solar and wind will be – I mean the total consequences – but I rarely get a clear answer. By now it is obvious that nuclear power has a lot of hidden costs. These are rarely calculated in by the lobbyists, but they become clear during and after installation; they include financial costs such as inevitable budget overruns, and environmental costs from all the cement and heavy construction equipment as well as the toxic waste products that no one knows how to dispose of. These "hidden costs" are becoming less and less hidden, more and more transparent, and that is one reason for nuclear power plants going out of favour. But what about the hidden costs of clean energy? No one has been able to provide me with a convincing case for why there aren't any.

An awful lot of steel goes into anchoring a giant wind turbine to the ground; construction and transportation requirements are considerable. What about decommissioning, how much of all this stuff can – or cannot – be recycled? Windmills often do not last as long as advertised. Many simply fall over and burn up. What about solar? Where are all the raw materials going to come from if we go from 5% to 100% renewable? The silicon, the aluminium, the copper. We will also need massive plants with batteries; as we know, the sun doesn't always shine and the wind doesn't always blow, so supply and demand have to be managed with giant storage facilities. Lithium for the batteries is already in short supply and so is cobalt, half of which is extracted using child labour in the Democratic Republic of Congo.[121] How ethical is that?

In my view, the jury is still out on many of these questions. However, if you wait for a perfect world before you move, you will never get anywhere. You have to put your capital to work. If you leave it at zero percent in the bank, asset price inflation and the 2% p.a. core CPI general price increases will eventually eat it up. How much did your parents pay for that house they live in? And how much would you have to pay to buy a similar one today? Quite likely 10 times as much. See what I mean? Look at the situation, do the best you can and pick a portfolio you feel good about.

If you settle for an ethical investment product such as an SRI mutual fund or ETF, clean energy companies will inevitably constitute a large component of that. And, provided you avoided the crash of 2008/2009, you would have enjoyed a reasonably decent return on a broad basket of these companies until now. Besides, to tweak the standard line included for all financial products: Mediocre returns in the past do not guarantee that returns in the future cannot be better! Once some consolidation has taken place within the clean energy industry, and the weak players have been shaken out, return on capital should improve. Sustainable power is a growing trend, and in spite of some of the issues I have highlighted, ethical investors should participate.

8

Positive Screening Options

"A business that makes nothing but money is a poor business."

— HENRY FORD

A constructive strategy

Remember the 10 positive screening themes from Chapter 5 (see page 88)? There were five grouped as environmental themes and five characterised as social themes. Those would be sectors and companies within the economy where ethical investors might be comfortable putting their hard-earned cash to work, while feeling good about themselves and hopefully earning a return on their investments – all at the same time. We just covered the biggest one – cleaner energy – in the previous chapter. That leaves nine others to consider; let us look at some of them in no particular order. Since the 10 ethical themes do not correspond anyway with the standard financial industry taxonomy – as it was developed by MSCI and Standard and Poor's – I will take the liberty here of tweaking their definition a bit along the way. What is important is that we develop a constructive investing strategy moving forward.

Like I stated earlier, as an investor you are looking for ways to make your capital grow. Personally I have come to believe that if we really want to save the planet, we have to move into an economic "de-growth" scenario where we reduce our population pressure and aggregate consumption. Either by choice or (more likely) by necessity, we will end up with a more circular and shared economy, as we covered in Chapter 3.

That is not to say that the so-called sharing economy business (SEB) is an automatic cure-all; it brings with it its own set of problems. In Singapore, ride-sharing services such as Uber and Grab were supposed to ease traffic congestion and reduce petrol consumption, but the opposite happened. After 2013 petrol consumption didn't fall as expected; it grew. Private citizens didn't share their own cars as intended; the companies involved registered hundreds of new vehicles and in effect just operated as competing taxi companies, except at a lower price, which increased demand and pulled customers away from public transport.

Moving by bicycle in the city is great and reduces pollution, but bike-sharing businesses such as Mobike, oBike and others generated heaps of garbage in the form of discarded bikes cluttering the environment. Specific to Singapore, in *Today Online*, Eric Teng wrote: "The raw materials used to produce each bicycle, for instance, can be put to better use, but as the business of bike-sharing continues to expand around the world, this will unlikely be happening. At the domestic level, the two-wheelers can be seen in clusters all over the island here, not being used and taking up space. In a study done by researchers from the Singapore-MIT Alliance for Research and Technology, they found that each of these dockless shared bicycles was used for merely half an hour a day... It is a form of wastage, so how can this enterprise be a solution to going green?"[122]

In a piece on the SEB, *Today Online* reported in 2018 about the room-sharing service Airbnb: "Other indirect costs are also often overlooked such as moral hazards and a deteriorating social fabric. For example, the sheer size of Airbnb's user base makes it next to impossible for platform owners or authorities to police undesirable social elements and criminal activities; the history of the firm is rife with social and legal abuses, ranging from racial discrimination, last-minute cancellations, money laundering, and bogus listings. The lack of regulation and enforcement on Airbnb's platform has also resulted in the illegal conversion of rentals into temporary brothels and drug dens."[123]

In spite of all this, I still believe that there will also be new areas of human activity and creativity where money can be made. As we saw in the beginning of this book, to make money in the future, and still preserve our standard of living and general welfare, we must conserve the financial and physical capital we have generated so far by exploiting the earth, and then channel it into restoration projects that will protect, conserve and enhance what little natural capital we have left.

In conventional economics, investors look for generally two types of growth: In the mature, high-income developed economies – mainly the OECD member countries – growth from here on forward will be technology-driven, so-called innovation growth. In developing countries – like India and China – there is so-called catch-up growth taking place.

Ecological economists such as Herman Daly believe that further conventional growth within mature economies is largely uneconomic. This is because industrial production has an element of disutility (cost) as well as utility (benefit). Daly points out in his work that at some stage during expansion, the marginal disutility of production in terms of overcapacity and associated pollution will exceed the marginal utility of further output. This renders further increase in output counterproductive, and the activity of perceived growth becomes uneconomic.[124] In developing countries, Daly concedes that there is still some welfare benefit to the catch-up growth, especially if distribution issues are addressed to reduce inequality in those societies. For both types of development stages, Herman Daly and other like-minded observers advocate an immediate move into a steady-state economy with de-growth of the primary extractive sectors and a circular and sustainable use of what has already been dug out. From a capital allocation point of view, it would be sufficient here to establish that there are indeed business areas where capital is needed going forward, and where ethical companies engaged in honest and decent activities will pay you a return on investment.

The eco-tourism explosion

So you want growth? You won't find a sector with more explosive growth than the eco-tourism business. This sector could fall into the quality-of-life theme, maybe with an element of knowledge (getting to know new places) and health (outdoor, hiking, etc). Look at the chart below and consider the enormous expansion that travel in general represents:

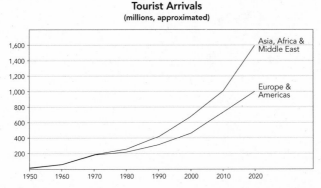

Tourist Arrivals
(millions, approximated)

When I was born in 1952, just a few million tourists travelled each year. Today it is well over 1 billion and rising. The graph shows the two major geographical regions. The top area is mainly for Asia; tourism numbers within Africa are still relatively small.

Right, most of these tourists don't care about the environment, of course. They just travel because they are bored at home and need a break. Thais come to Singapore to shop and eat, and Singaporeans go to Thailand to shop and eat – that sort of thing.

But a lot of them do care; they want to see nature and animals and experience the great outdoors.

I spent a couple of months in Iceland in the summer of 1973; I walked across the island from the north to the south, but I didn't see many people there. When I got to the Haukadalur Valley, where the proper road south back to Reykjavik started, there were a few other tourists looking at the Geysir hot springs. But no one in those days ever considered going to look at whales – why would you do that? The chart below shows the tourists going to Iceland – more than 20% of them now go there to watch whales!

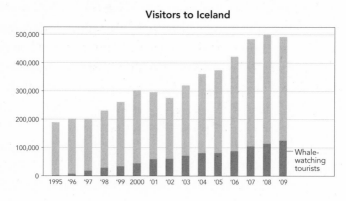

Visitors to Iceland

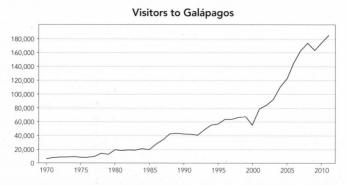

Visitors to Galápagos

I think it would be safe to classify everyone going to the Galápagos Islands off Ecuador's mainland as such eco-tourists. Notice a similar explosive growth in tourist arrivals during the last four decades or so. The two drops in the curve correspond to drops in the global stock markets!

As an ethical investor, maybe you want to encourage eco-tourism, and maybe you want to capitalise on the growth in that "industry" as well. After all, isn't it nice that the public shows an interest in and appreciates nature? Many surveys show that small-scale eco-tourism projects benefit the local rural economy much more than do mass-market urban tourism schemes. The problem for the investor is that it might be difficult to distinguish between authentic, environmentally friendly eco-tourism and conventional mass-market travel, which you might not feel so comfortable promoting or even being associated with. After all, while it was previously believed that tourism accounted for 2% of global GHG emissions, new studies show that the figure is in fact 8%.[125]

Also, in general, in spite of incredible growth in the air travel industry in the past few decades, airlines have often not been a good investment. The business is pervaded with opaque government regulations and market-distorting subsidies; the industry is also not particularly green. While many general hotel chains and hospitality projects are listed or included in REITs available to small investors, pure eco-tourism ventures are rarely listed on the stock exchanges, so buying a share might not be easy. Although growing rapidly and potentially profitable, this sector might be better suited for small private business ventures and private equity investors.

The darker side of travel

We cannot leave the eco-tourism topic without highlighting its dark side. It sometimes appears as if we are loving nature to death. On a small scale, here in Singapore, I used to go to the Bukit Timah Nature Reserve in the 1980s and more often than not I would be the only person there. There was a small car park on a patch of dirt at the bottom of the hill, and if there was another car there I would wonder who that might be. Today hundreds of people visit every day; during weekends, thousands. The large new car park is full every Sunday morning, and cars are parked illegally along Hindhede Drive down to Upper Bukit Timah Road. But the reserve is feeling the heat. Trails are overused, the large trees are falling, gaps in the canopy are appearing, and instead of the song of birds all you hear are people chatting away. In 2016–2017 the reserve had to be closed to the public for a year, just to give the forest a break to recover.

On a larger scale, this is happening in most eco-tourism destinations. Increasingly the protected areas around the world are turning into shrinking pockets of biodiversity that are struggling to cope with the human pressure. The buffer zones are being eaten into by development and encroachments from settlers, the core areas invaded and disrupted by eco-visitors, well-meaning as most of those are. In East Africa, the small remaining game reserves are increasingly acting like open zoos, where the rangers know the name of each iconic animal there – while the surrounding areas are denuded and stripped bare by overpopulation, drought and deforestation. Look at this chart from Mauritius in the Indian Ocean, a popular destination for divers, snorkellers and other eco-tourists:

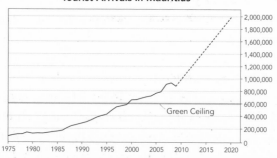

Tourist Arrivals in Mauritius

Sorry, eco-travellers, Paradise is full up! The threshold for sustainable visitor arrivals to Mauritius has already been exceeded, according to welovemauritius.org.[126]

This is happening all over the world. The wonderful nature destinations simply cannot deal with all of us. In 2018, Boracay Island in the Philippines had to be closed to visitors on orders from President Duterte, who said that the island had become an overcrowded "cesspool".[127]

The welovemauritius.org site puts it this way: "Even eco-tourism projects have a negative environmental impact." It is one of the paradoxes of our time that as the interest in nature and the outdoors is exploding, nature itself is imploding. The American/Canadian environmentalist Rex Weyler says: "Today, we have more environmental groups and less forest, more 'protected areas' and less species, more carbon taxes and greater carbon emissions, more 'green' products and less green space."[128] It seems we have to go back to my favourite LTA quote from Chapter 7 and conclude: The greenest eco-tourist is one that does not exist.

Environmental services

As I have mentioned before, it is likely that more and more resources – labour and capital – will have to be allocated to environmental protection and restoration going forward. These activities will include cleaning operations, waste collection plus treatment and disposal, material recovery and recycling, as well as safety and health safeguards. Many businesses are involved in all this. Some are large listed companies with decent earnings; helping them with capital would be a satisfying – as well as potentially profitable – undertaking.

You can check your local stock exchange and source for companies you like in this space; in places like Singapore and China there are some, and in the US there are many more. Take a field like water supply. Many countries – and especially cities – suffer from water shortages due to overpopulation and overconsumption. The fact that many large corporations (Nestlé comes to mind, but there are others[129]) suck up the limited – free – water at source and then put it into plastic bottles and sell it back to the local residents at a dollar per shot hasn't helped, but we will leave this issue aside here. In 2018, Cape Town in South Africa officially became the first major city to start shutting off its water supply completely as it approached "day zero"; and it won't be the last – Sao Paulo, Brazil; Jakarta, Indonesia; and Mexico City, Mexico, are not far behind.[130] The World Resources Institute has warned of the rise in water stress globally, "with 33 countries projected to face extreme high stress in 2040".[131] Researchers with Aarhus University in Denmark expect that 30–40% of the world's population will be affected by water shortages by 2020.

Yes, you can find solutions; you can recycle sewage, desalinate sea water, etc. – Singapore does all that. But it is going to cost you. These measures don't come cheap, and the poor countries will not be able to afford them. My cousin has a cottage in Sweden, a holiday home for him and his family; when they need water they go down to the creek and scoop up a few pails of it. It doesn't cost them anything and doesn't add anything to the Swedish GDP numbers. The rest of us will have to pay for water through the nose in the future. In Singapore, a cubic metre of potable water costs S$1.21, but after the waterborne fee, conservation tax and sales tax are added, the price is S$2.93 – more than double! And it is only going to go up from here. We consumers are not better off, but the GDP figures will grow and make us look nice and rich.

Which companies will benefit? Like with the wind turbine industry, this is hard to say. So if you are not sure about picking individual stocks, spread your risk over a basket of them or find an SRI mutual fund or ETF with exposure to this sector. In Singapore, we have at least 20 companies listed on the SGX doing exactly that: providing environmental services – and especially water treatment facilities – to market participants in Singapore, China and the rest of Asia. *The Edge* did a feature on five of them in 2017.[132] CITIC Envirotech has been a great investment if you got in early, but otherwise check with a financial adviser you trust, or do your own fundamental analysis if you have the time, before you buy in.

Other ethical sectors

You know the three Rs, right? Reduce, reuse and recycle. In my view, it is always better to use the first one: simply use less. That doesn't do much to pump up our nominal GDP numbers, but it does a great deal to not wreck the earth and to improve our personal well-being and general welfare overall. By reducing our economic and environmental footprint, we preserve not only natural, but also financial, capital. This will help us become financially free so much sooner.

As a last resort, yes, we should reuse and recycle as much of our stuff as we can. In Singapore, we have companies listed on the main board which do that: recycle materials. They are EcoWise Holdings Ltd and Enviro-Hub Holdings Ltd; both have struggled to make money lately, but if you get them at a good price they are ethical investments you can sleep well at night owning. Go through your own local stock exchange listings for similar companies and check them out.

On the US exchanges there are numerous great companies that do decent things. I will not make individual stock recommendations here; there are plenty of other places you can find this chatter. For me, I have from time to time held some companies involved in recycling materials, energy conservation and healthy lifestyle choices; they have done well for me, although I am currently out of the American market altogether because I think it is overpriced and there are better opportunities elsewhere at the moment.

In Singapore I have shares in a few healthcare companies, such as Religare Health Trust and Raffles Medical Group; they have done OK and provide me with a bit of dividend income. Personally

I am a bit sceptical about much of what goes on in the health-care business; I suspect not all of it is that ethical. Many reports reveal that a lot of unnecessary tests and treatments as well as over-prescription of painkillers, antibiotics and other medication take place, facilitated mainly by an unscrupulous pharmaceutical and health insurance industry. However, healthcare is part of the established ethical investing positive screening themes, and based on my own fairly limited personal experience I think most doctors are fine people who do their best. So in general I am OK with these investments. However, I never buy into insurance companies directly, exactly for ethical reasons; in my opinion those function as reverse gambling enterprises. (I will just leave it at that here; feel free to consult *Be Financially Free* for a detailed discussion of the insurance industry.)

General quality-of-life products and services – including education and knowledge – are some of the other positive screening themes that would be acceptable to most ethical investors. We looked at the eco-tourism segment before; associated with that is the whole outdoor lifestyle and education sphere. I don't think there is any downside to education – we can never get enough of that, and there are several private tuition centres that you can buy into. I have been fortunate to have been involved in various nature businesses, promoting knowledge and appreciation of birds and animals and plants and ecology. Did you know that according to the American Birding Association there are 47 million birdwatchers in the US above 16 years old? Sure, most of those (88%) are casual backyard birders, but they count too. The 2011 survey found that American birdwatchers spent $41 billion that year – $15 billion on trips and $26 billion on equipment. Total yearly birding output, including an economic multiplier effect: $107 billion. The business provides a staggering 666,000 jobs to the economy, more than all the green energy projects combined.[133] The market for healthy leisure activities and knowledge is colossal.

Technology... I can't help but notice that holdings in Microsoft Corp, Apple Inc, Intel Corp and other technology favourites are part and parcel of most SRI mutual funds that you might be considering buying into. Sure, these names have grown nicely in value lately and as such they add to portfolio performance and overall returns. But ethical? Compared to nuclear weapons manufacturers, I guess most technology companies don't do that much harm – though some of their business customs have turned out to be ethically questionable: monopolistic practices, production sweatshops in poorly regulated countries, self-destruct features in new equipment leading to waste, that sort of thing.

The same goes for the "sustainable property" theme. What is so sustainable about building more skyscrapers and condos? Sure, some property developers try to pay careful attention to the environment, and that is all very nice. But I believe we can tweak the LTA statement one more time and state: The greenest building is one that does not exist! REITs (real estate investment trusts) are popular with retail investors because they pay high dividends – they have to, by law, as that is one of the mandated features of a trust as opposed to a regular incorporated property company. However, REITs have also come under some scrutiny. Their very structure encourages short-term profiteering; tenants are squeezed to pay ever higher rents. Nevertheless, yes, I do buy a few shares in REITs to supplement my passive income; I can live with that, although I do not find them particularly sustainable. All the same, it is my view that if you insist on a perfect world before you move, you will never get anywhere.

The biofuels fiasco

Before we leave the positive screening themes, how about the food sector? By right this should be a morally strong and principled segment providing tasty and nutritious food to the world at a competitive price. If you dig into it, it might not always be the case.

Firstly, somewhat related to the food sector, there is the bio-fuels debacle. It sounded good on paper some decades ago, when it was suggested that we could make plant matter into fuel. Finally we had the magic wand we had always been looking for. We could grow all the fuel we needed in a sustainable manner and burn it off in combustion engines, then by planting new crops we would just re-absorb all the CO_2 released – clever, right? Unfortunately it didn't work out that way. Check out this paper from 2008 with the telling title: "N_2O release from agro-biofuel production negates global warming reduction by replacing fossil fuels."[134] It was found in America that producing ethanol from corn as a substitute for petroleum-based gasoline used up more power than was generated.

Biofuels generally come in two forms: ethanol from plant matter used in petrol engines; and so-called "green diesel" made from vegetable oil crops like rapeseed oil (Europe), soybean (the Americas) and palm oil (Asia). Heavily subsidised to the tune of billions of Euros annually, the production and use of biofuels increased in the EU during the 2000s and 2010s; one single litre of ethanol biofuel is subsidised with EUR0.74; that is about half the price of a litre of petrol at the pump in most EU countries![135] Incredibly, fuel oil is imported into the EU in large quantities from Indonesia, where the palm oil industry is notorious for causing devastating deforestation, social unrest among displaced villagers and regular plantation burning exercises, the haze from which poisons the air over much of Southeast Asia during dry spells.[136]

In more general terms, biofuels encourage industrial farming using excessive amounts of fertilisers, herbicides and pesticides – and they drain not only peat swamp forests but also public funds, as they require state subsidies to compete economically. A report in sciencemag.org concluded: "Converting rainforests, peatlands, savannas, or grasslands to produce food crop-based biofuels in Brazil, Southeast Asia, and the US creates a 'biofuel carbon debt' by releasing 17 to 420 times more CO_2 than the annual GHG reductions that these biofuels would provide by replacing fossil fuels."[137] Apart from that, by removing food crops from the markets, biofuels have also contributed to increases in food prices and associated social problems, such as the food riots that started the so-called Arab Spring in 2011. Growing food to burn it in engines turned out to be not such a brilliant idea after all.

Could the biofuel business have some merits for the ethical investor? Maybe. The same report that I quoted above also writes: "Biofuels made from waste biomass or from biomass grown on degraded and abandoned agricultural lands planted with perennials incur little or no carbon debt and can offer immediate and sustained GHG advantages." So if your SRI collective investment product includes some biofuel or "green diesel" components, look into this and consider how green they really are.

Staying with the palm oil aspect of this, more than anything else this particular commodity has contributed to environmental damage and controversy here in Southeast Asia where I am based. I have lost count of the conferences we have had here trying to pave a way forward for a sustainable palm oil industry. Kudos to everyone involved in this. Of course the greenest palm oil plantation is one that does not exist, and in fact a 2016 WWF report looked at the potential impact of replacing palm oil throughout Germany with other vegetable oils. Unfortunately the report concluded that this would only serve to shift and possibly exacerbate the problems with land use, carbon emissions and biodiversity loss.[138]

Remember the advertising campaign a few years ago (running around 2014–2015): "When the buying stops, the killing can too"? Various organisations opposing animal poaching, shark's fin harvesting and illegal wildlife trade introduced this slogan, and I think it could apply to palm oil as well: When the buying stops, the deforestation can too. We can encourage the big wholesale buyers – Unilever, Nestlé, PepsiCo, Mars – to avoid harmful products; or better still, as consumers we can avoid them ourselves. And as investors we might want to stop buying investments with exposure to the plantation sector; it is the only way.

The things we eat

This is not an ethical consumer guide; there are plenty of those out there already. I enjoyed reading Mark Brassington's *How To Go Carbon Neutral* (2008), although I realise that some of his advice is not really practical – not everyone can power their home with woodchips, and personally I don't think feeding on roadkill will catch on anytime soon (I am not kidding, Brassington suggests that!). But there are other things we can do individually as consumers and investors to ensure a better lifestyle for ourselves and a better planet for everyone in general. And one important one relates to our food, especially our consumption of meat.

It is widely documented that meat production is one of the most ecologically harmful activities we humans engage in. Cutting down pristine rainforest to raise cattle is diabolical, yet it is done on a massive scale in South and Central America, where more than 20,000 sq km of forest is cleared every year for that purpose, half the size of the Netherlands. It takes 12 kg of grain and almost 10,000 litres of water to produce 1 kg of beef. Some 70% of American grain is used – or misused – on feeding livestock.[139] The waste products from domesticated animals pollute our fields and waterways and even our air. In the US, manure from farm animals amounts to roughly 10 times the waste from the human population. If we all stopped eating meat, our agricultural footprint on Earth could be reduced by 75% – that is an area equivalent to the US, China, EU and Australia, combined![140]

And that is not considering the animal cruelty aspects of this. Anyone who has looked into the conditions of industrial-scale feedlots and battery chickens living in the dark with legs so weak that they cannot hold up their bloated bodies would agree that something here is not right. Or the health difficulties we have with the so-called zoonotic diseases transferring from animals into humans – swine flu, bird flu, foot-and-mouth disease, salmonellosis, ebola virus, HIV, brucellosis... the list goes on. Red meats pumped up with steroids, antibiotics and growth hormones and later treated with nitrates have been linked to heart disease, high blood pressure, diabetes, obesity and some cancers in humans.[141]

As you might have noticed, personally I don't think there is any easy way out of our ecological dilemmas – that is why I advise you to prepare for calamity ahead. Heck, I cannot even stop eating meat myself! I love a juicy beefburger, and like most people I just close my eyes to how that beef is actually being made. However, if anyone could come up with a better alternative, well, I would be interested. Enter the organic farming industry and, even better, meatless meat. Yes, the jury is still out debating whether this term is legally acceptable, but meatless meat and organic produce is definitely a growth industry. According to eco-business.com: "Meatless meat is attracting serious investment. Singapore-based company Temasek recently [2018] co-led two investment rounds worth over US$180 million in US-based plant protein innovator, Impossible Foods, which has expansion plans for Hong Kong and Singapore." And: "Newly launched Dao Foods International aspires to disrupt the global meat market by driving plant-based protein and clean meat expansion in China. The Asian market, with its big population, growing middle class, and increasing meat consumption has investors licking their lips with anticipation."[142]

Pig-free bacon, cow-free beef, chicken-free chicken are on their way into our supermarkets. There they will join a host of other organic and fair-trade products on the shelves vying for the attention and pocketbooks of the new political consumer. Will the fad take hold? The richest man in the world, Jeff Bezos, seems to think so. He runs Amazon.com Inc, of course, and has been pretty successful at that, you must admit. Amazon bought Whole

Foods Market Inc in 2017, an American supermarket chain with 479 stores renowned for their ecological stance on produce. Whole Foods specialises in organic products with no artificial additives such as sweeteners, colours, flavours and hydrogenated fats; they do not sell eggs from battery-cage chickens; they insist on labelling for GMO products and seafood from controversial fish farms; they also encourage humane treatment of animals and reduction of plastic use. When Temasek Holdings and Amazon.com get in on new trends like these, it may pay off for other investors to pay attention.

9

The Ethical Portfolio

*"There is nothing wrong with being well off
as long as money has a social
and ethical value."*

— AGA KHAN IV

Asset allocation

In the previous chapters we established the basics for an ethical investment scheme. We identified sectors and companies that you might want to avoid; we also looked for themes and companies that you might want to include. By putting your money to work in an ethical – rather than an unethical – manner, you will not only feel better about yourself and be happier, you will also help to build a better world, and on top of that – if you get your strategy right – you will make more money. What is there about ethical investing not to like?

Like with all investing, there are some important concepts that you have to consider, the foremost being your allocation over asset classes. It is generally recommended in the financial industry that you have a combination of shares and fixed income products in your portfolio. What the ratio should be is a personal choice; no two portfolios will ever be exactly the same. If you take your cue from some of the big boys, notice that the Government of Singapore Investment Corporation (GIC) in 2015 had an asset allocation ratio of 47% shares, 37% fixed income (bonds), 7% real estate and 9% private equity.[143] The similar – but somewhat larger – Government Pension Fund of Norway aims for a slightly more aggressive 70:30 shares/bonds ratio. At the other extreme you have Warren Buffett, probably the most successful investor in the world: He advises that you put 90% of your money into a mutual fund or an ETF tracking the S&P 500 index and 10% in government treasuries.

What ratio is right for you will depend partly on your investment horizon. It has been said that your percentage of share holdings should be 100 minus your age. So if you are 40 years old, you should keep 100 - 40 = 60% of your portfolio in shares, the rest in fixed income. However, some of us might have a higher appetite for risk than others. If you can except more risk, increase your holdings of stocks. You should also be aware that by diversifying you are generally better protected during market downturns. In a recession scenario, stocks and property tend to drop in value while interest rates typically decline as well, sending bond prices higher. But the flip side of that is that a diversified portfolio tends to increase less during the good times. Wealthy people rarely diversify as advised; they take great risks and some get rewarded – usually those you hear about in the news, the rest just fade into obscurity! Buffett himself doesn't follow his own advice: He doesn't buy the index; he picks individual stocks and has been very good at it.

In the 1980s I did well personally, not by diversifying but by piling all my funds into high-yield mortgage-backed fixed income securities that were paying 16–22% yield per annum at the time. None of them ever defaulted. I geared my portfolio further by borrowing in low-interest currencies and investing more in those high-yield products. This is called the carry trade; you can still do it today but not nearly as effectively. Yes, if you had borrowed in Euros during 2017 and invested in USD you would have had an interest rate advantage of maybe 2%, but that same year the dollar dropped from 1.05 to 1.20 to the EURO (a drop of some 14%), so all in all you would have lost out big! In the latter half of the 1980s it was different – the interest rate differential that I took advantage of at the time between USD (borrow) and DKK (invest) was substantial and included a currency windfall – and as you can imagine, my capital grew rapidly in an exponential manner, which made me financially independent within a few years. I would not recommend this strategy to others today, but sometimes you might just get lucky if you keep an eye out for opportunities. Yes, I said lucky. I don't believe in gambling, but I do believe in taking some calculated risks in life – in luck, if you will. But I also agree with the guy who said: "I believe in luck. It just seems that the harder I work, the luckier I get!"

Anyone who had an overweight in technology shares in their stock portfolio during the 2010s would have done really well. However, identifying the individual winners in this space would not have been so easy. Who could predict back in the 2000s that Facebook would outcompete MySpace (backed by Rupert Murdoch himself), that Google would beat Yahoo hands down, that Apple would make Nokia virtually obsolete or that loss-making Amazon would annihilate the main-street retail sector as we know it? I certainly could not. Technology winners are easy to see in hindsight, not so easy to spot during the development stage. So unless you have vital inside information or are an exceedingly wealthy private equity investor, maybe you had better stick to an ETF tracking technology stocks or another sector you like, rather than try to select individual growth companies.

If you do try to outsmart the market, take heart in the fact that you do not have to be super-smart to do so. In fact, many surveys show that high-IQ people do pretty poorly investing! This might fly in the face of common sense, but you cannot deny the facts. In 2018, *Today Online* published an interesting piece showing that the top – presumably super-smart – investment advisers with Harvard University's endowment fund took a $1.1 billion write-down on their natural resources holdings during 2015 – yet the seven managers in question were paid a total of $58 million for their performance that year. Over a 10-year period from 2008 to 2017, these Harvard geniuses managed a compounded return of 4.35% p.a. – compared to a "dumb" 60:40 allocation ratio adjusted annually (a so-called Gone Fishin' portfolio; see *Be Financially Free* for details) which would have yielded 6.77% p.a. over the same period – over 50% more money![144]

This article also quotes from a study of Mensa members and their investment club. Mensa is of course that egg-head organisation open only to people with IQ scores in the top 2% of the population. For the 15-year period from 1986 to 2001, the Mensa investment club managed to get an average return of 2.5% annually versus the 15.3% annual return of the S&P 500 index. This doesn't automatically mean that all smart people are bad investors. It just means that you have to take the "expert" opinions out there with a grain of salt. You might have heard of the $1 million bet Warren Buffett made in 2007 against a basket of hedge funds selected by asset management firm Protege Partners. That bet ended in 2017; the hedge funds returned 2.2% p.a. compounded, while Buffett's preferred S&P 500 index fund returned 7.1% compounded yearly. Smart versus dumb investing – no contest at all!

Portfolio balancing

Diversification is not just about spreading your exposure over various asset classes and business sectors; it is also about diversifying geographically and across the major currencies. Try to have exposure to both emerging markets and mature economies, and tweak your allocation to fit your own outlook and the advice of financial observers that you trust. A varied mixture of assets will protect you against so-called unsystematic risk, i.e. risk specific to certain companies or sectors; but even a well-diversified portfolio will take a hit when the financial markets crash and all asset classes contract for a while as the big investors scramble for safety and go into cash and short-term money market funds. But you will most likely get hit less hard if you have a wider exposure; and provided that you don't borrow, you will be able to recoup and recover when everyone else does, after the recession is over.

Here are a few ways to balance your portfolio according to your appetite for risk and your general temperament and interests:

1. **The aggressive/speculative portfolio**: A selection of "high-beta" stocks, with an overweight of small-cap companies and newly listed firms. High-beta stocks ($\beta > 1$) move up and down more than the market in general. This type of portfolio would only suit high-risk individuals or people with a long time horizon, such as young people with a large regular income.

2. **The defensive portfolio**: Low-beta and non-cyclical stocks. Non-cyclical stocks produce or distribute stuff we always need, such as power, water and essential household non-durable goods; such shares tend to drop less during a recession. Suitable for investors with low tolerance for risk.

3. **The income portfolio**: An overweight of high-dividend shares such as mature blue-chips, REITs and business trusts that pay high annual dividends. But please consider that these companies typically have less share price upside potential, as they have to maintain a high dividend payout ratio and therefore retain less capital for expansion; also they are typically late in the business cycle and could be about to become obsolete. Therefore this type of portfolio

is suitable mainly for elderly rentiers and retirees who need a regular capital income and who are less concerned about capital gains.

4. **The hybrid portfolio**: A combination of index stocks, bonds, some commodities and other asset classes. Highly diversified mix that is suitable for long-term investors such as pension funds, sovereign wealth funds and individuals who just check their holdings a few times a year.

To expand on defensive portfolios, many surveys confirm repeatedly that certain business sectors are more recession-proof than others. Although each downturn is unique, it is possible to conclude that the risk-adverse investor is able to safeguard his portfolio somewhat by avoiding the very cyclical sectors and maintaining an overweight of the defensive ones. If we look at the Great Recession – the biggest global financial crisis we have had so far in my lifetime – this chart tracks the global equity correction from 12 October 2007 to the market bottom on 6 March 2009 according to sector:

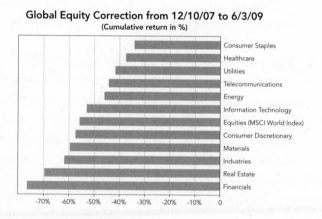

Global Equity Correction from 12/10/07 to 6/3/09
(Cumulative return in %)

Notice that while world equities as a whole fell by 56% during that period, the consumer staples segment fell by a lot less, only 34%. Healthcare, utilities and telecommunications were other defensive sectors, while financials and real estate were the hardest hit.

Broad or core SRI?

Keeping these allocation issues in mind, for the ethical investor there is the additional factor of SRI to consider, i.e. the social, sustainable and responsible aspects of your portfolio. I get it, most of us are mainly concerned about bread-and-butter issues: we just want a decent return on our capital and to live in financial freedom. However, I am convinced you can achieve that goal and still have a clear conscience, knowing that you do the right thing.

I am aware that for each opinion there is a counter-opinion, and there are advisers out there who will urge you to invest in so-called sin stocks for the great return they provide. There are several books in the market with titles such as *Stocking Up on Sin* and *Investing in Vice: The Recession-Proof Portfolio of Booze, Bets, Bombs & Butts*. I mean, I have a sense of humour, but I just don't find bombing people and encouraging others to live a life in gambling debt all that funny. And since you have bought this book – and not one of the others – I suppose you agree with me somewhat.

In ethical investing, advisers distinguish between broad SRI and core SRI. In the broad version, you apply some general ethical considerations, a bit like some of the big institutional investors we covered in Chapter 5, i.e. you might negatively screen out certain offensive companies, but otherwise accept most of the market as it is. As we have seen, today there are so many ethical investment products available – mutual funds and ETFs with a declared ESG and/or SRI policy. Look carefully at those you might consider and go through their holdings closely. Then ask yourself, can I accept this combination of companies?

THE ETHICAL INVESTOR'S HANDBOOK

Depending on how much time you want to spend, there are tons of research tools for this purpose online. I enjoyed reading the report "Environmental Markets: A New Asset Class" (2014) by the CFA Institute Research Foundation; it is a bit US-centric, but you will find very precise and competent advice on how to understand and navigate the ESG investment field; there is even a chapter on "Building a Sustainable Portfolio".[145] Most likely – depending on where you are based – you might not want to buy into those particular funds featured, but it is useful to look at them and go through their holdings to compare with ESG/SRI funds that your own bank or financial adviser might suggest. Virtually all the big mutual fund and ETF providers have products with the SRI, ethical or just ESG label; they are all pouring into this space to take advantage of the increase in demand from institutional and private investors. Find a fund that you trust and that you are comfortable with.

If you cannot find a collective investment product you are happy with, then you might have to move into a core SRI position. That involves more ruthless positive screening, in other words you select only specific companies that you like and avoid all the others, including banks that help finance them and retail companies that sell their products. Refer back to the table in Chapter 5 (page 85) and remind yourself what values are important to you. Say you are truly alarmed about global warming, then most ESG ETFs will probably not be good enough for you. They are likely to have companies with dual activities in them, as well as financial institutions making all of it possible. Or you could be a human rights advocate, in which case most multinational corporations would be unacceptable to you with their lax oversight of Third World suppliers that have people working in abhorrent conditions. In this case, you could not buy most index funds – they would quite likely have Apple Inc, Nestlé S.A. or Shell Plc in them, as well as many other MNCs with dubious human rights records.

So the core SRI investor would in reality have to construct his or her own ethical portfolio. It is not as hard as it sounds. There are already fund managers who apply a "smart beta" strategy, and the serious ethical investor could do something similar. Smart beta means that you approach a selection of stocks and exclude those that you think will be a drag on returns going forward. In other words, you tweak the composition of the portfolio to suit your outlook. With an ethical mindset, you would exclude those that operate against your principles but include those that you agree with, to a lesser or greater extent. Just remember that the world is not perfect, and it probably never will be. But try to do the best you can.

Build your own ethical fund

Personally I was faced with this dilemma in 2013 when I received a windfall, a small inheritance from my mother's estate; she died in December 2012. My mother lived in Denmark and did business with Danske Bank, so out of respect I kept my share of her money there, transferred into my name once my sister had settled all my late mother's affairs. It was not an option to keep cash, and yield on fixed income in Danish kroners (DKK) was ridiculously low to non-existent at the time, due to the ECB's monetary policy of negative deposit rates and huge assets purchases that I have mentioned earlier (page 46). So I had to buy shares, and I only wanted shares included in the OMX Copenhagen 20 (C20) index of blue-chips listed on the Copenhagen stock exchange. I simply did a broad ethical smart beta selection according to my own preference, and set up a small portfolio that I still hold on to. I use the dividends to pay for airline tickets for my sons so that we can all meet up once in a while – the way I imagine that my mother would have wanted me to.

Of the 20 companies in the C20, I ruled out oil and transport companies such as Maersk and DSV and also companies involved in chemicals and construction. But I did include the major banks, although those might not be strictly ethical. I did that as a hedge: I figured that bank stocks were somewhat correlated with the property market in the sense that they should go up if the property market did, and that way I would be somewhat protected against price increases should I ever want to move back to Scandinavia and buy a home there (which appears increasingly unlikely today!). Otherwise I simply positively screened in the other few companies that I liked and could accept being associated with – names such as Vestas Wind Systems (wind turbines), Novo Nordisk (a well-managed pharmaceutical company), Genmap (cancer treatment) and TDC (telecommunications; the company was later privatised). Will my smart beta selection beat the benchmark, which would of course be the C20 index as a whole? I don't quite know about that yet, but I know I feel better this way!

So find your own local index, be it the S&P 500 in the States (the Dow Jones Industrial with only 30 stocks is just too narrow for this purpose), the STI index in Singapore, the FTSE 100 in the UK, or the ASX 200 in Australia. Then tweak the index the ethical smart beta way and set up your own broad ESG/SRI fund.

Be aware, though, that if you move out from this fairly safe policy into core SRI practises, you have to accept that your overall risk most likely increases as well. Green or strictly ethical businesses – somewhat by definition – put less emphasis on profit at all cost; this makes them simply more vulnerable. That is a sad fact of life. There are many opportunities to invest in core ethical companies, especially smaller-capitalisation firms and start-ups. Just understand that many of those companies might not pay a dividend for many years, if ever, and many will not make it over the long haul at all.

Then we are into the venture capital/angel investor scenario, which is a little bit outside the scope of this book. If you are brave enough for this milieu, consider the crowd-funding option. There are many crowd-funding sites available online, and who knows, maybe you can make a buck and do good at the same time by helping out some guys (or gals) with a brilliant idea but who just cannot get a conventional loan at the bank.

Here is a case from real life. I have always thought that it is crazy that we still use plastic wrapping and styrofoam containers for packaging when biodegradable paper and containers have been available for decades. When a local Singapore company put up a post on one of the crowd-funding sites to fund a new venture to produce and market cornstalk-based food containers and packaging to supermarkets and food courts, I thought it sounded like a sure-win. The company offered 20% p.a. return on a S$100,000 tranche of capital, payable back within six months. My wife talked me out of helping them, and she was probably right. There was little guarantee that I would ever get my money back; however, I never followed up on this, so I cannot tell you how that venture panned out for the start-up. But I can tell you that I have never seen their products at our local supermarket or anywhere else.

An economist would pull his hair in desperation that something like this cannot be done – the introduction of biodegradable packaging – considering the astronomical costs embedded in our addiction to plastic. But that is the usual problem of our market economy being unable to calculate in the external environmental costs of operations. This is the so-called tragedy of the commons. We destroy our air, our public lands and our oceans because stuff like that doesn't have a price.

A UN report from 2015 found that almost no industry is actually profitable if environmental costs are included. To quote from the summary that came out at the time: "The report found that when you took the externalised costs into effect, essentially NONE of the industries was actually making a profit. The huge profit margins being made by the world's most profitable industries (oil, meat, tobacco, mining, electronics) is being paid

The tragedy of the commons

Since the "tragedy of the commons" concept is often referred to in ecological economics, and since it goes to the heart of sustainability issues, let me briefly explain the theory. The expression was first put forward by a British economist who way back in 1833 published an essay where he identified a problem with open-access land, the so-called commons. This was open pasture land near a village, and since all villagers had equal access, they all wanted their cows to graze there as much as possible. None of them had an interest in conserving the grasslands, and this led to over-exploitation, and the land eventually become worthless.

The concept was forgotten for a while but was picked up again in 1968, when the American ecologist Garrett Hardin used it to describe a more general problem with shared and unregulated "free" resources such as the atmosphere, oceans, rivers and forests. Since then it has been expanded to explain even the littering of shared public spaces.

The idea of a resource being communally owned might initially appear appealing, but it can have dire unintended consequences. For instance, our atmosphere is free for everyone to use; nice, right? Yes, but a factory will benefit from belching black smoke into it, while another factory installing chimney filters will have a severe competitive disadvantage and go bankrupt; so ultimately this mechanism will prove catastrophic and encourage a race to the bottom. Hardin established that perverse incentives to overuse the commons inescapably led to ecological disaster and collapse of the common resources. He later followed up with a book entitled *Living Within Limits* (1993), in which he tried to find solutions to this conundrum.

Hardin regarded the growth of the human population – encouraged by the welfare state, economists and other people he collectively labelled "growthmaniacs" – as the greatest tragedy of the commons of them all.

Other observers have argued that the only escape out of this calamity appears to be to regulate the use of the commons and to put a price on something that is otherwise free, either through government legislation and international treaties, or – where appropriate – through privatisation. But this is easier said than done, and after 50 years of pondering over this, ecological economists are still busy discussing among themselves how to go about all this – while the commons themselves are being exploited like crazy, worse than ever before.

for against the future: we are trading long-term sustainability for the benefit of shareholders. Sometimes the environmental costs vastly outweighed revenue, meaning that these industries would be constantly losing money had they actually been paying for the ecological damage and strain they were causing."[146] But of course they don't actually pay for the damage; they just dump their waste at no cost somewhere into the commons and forget about it. But in my opinion, we have to find a way out of this conundrum and well, hopefully one day, when my teenage son is out of college and my ship comes in, I can get into hardcore do-gooder investing to find solutions; for now, my wife and I cannot afford the risk associated with this kind of social or impact investing.

I have found that it will help you a bit when you search for ways to put your capital to work if you follow your heart. That might sound like a bit of a contradiction – I always say that finance and investing should not be emotional, it is all about the cold hard numbers. But that might not always be the case. And Patricia Aburdene see eye to eye with me on this one; in *Conscious Money* she writes: "Combining head and heart can be the basis for making good investment choices." Aburdene urges us to identify our passion (or passions) in life – things we care deeply about – and invest in those sectors. It could be that you are passionate about education, music, food or technology. In that case you are also likely to know a lot about that area, and "that wisdom and expertise may later help you make sound investments", Aburdene writes. "Of course you must balance what you know about that passion with reliable financial data and solid investing advice." Absolutely!

Can do-gooders make a buck?

Finally, we cannot leave this chapter without addressing the question that's always on everyone's mind: Can ethical investing make money? Having studied this, I believe that with regard to ROI

– return on investment – ethical investing is not that much different from all other kinds of investing. Some portfolios will pay off, others will be less profitable. We saw already in Chapter 6 how the Government Pension Fund Global of Norway is doing pretty well. Is that because of its declared SRI view or in spite of it? Either way you look at it, there is no doubt that the two – ethical policies and stellar returns – can be brought together with the right fund management.

An article in *Today Online* (28 April 2018) confirms this: "Research has shown that socially responsible companies produce higher returns and have lower risks. A study of more than 2,000 research projects by Deutsche Bank, for instance, found that the business case for ESG investing is empirically well-founded. The positive ESG impact appears stable over time regardless of region or asset class, such as emerging markets, corporate bonds, and green real estate. Investment manager Pimco similarly said that sustainable investing makes good business sense because it can help mitigate risks and potentially improve the return profile of an investment portfolio. And investment firm Pax found growing evidence that integrating ESG factors into investment analysis and portfolio construction offers investors potential long-term performance advantages. Looking more specifically at mutual funds, financial services giant Morgan Stanley found that nearly two-thirds of sustainable equity mutual funds had higher returns and lower volatility compared to other funds. Moreover, it said numerous studies have found lower risk and outperformance for portfolios that integrated ESG factors alongside rigorous financial analysis."

The article goes on to explain the connection between ethics and returns: "The reasons for that superior performance are straightforward. Companies that treat employees and customers well, reduce waste and follow other socially responsible practices can produce more attractive products, lower costs, benefit from more productive employees, and more – all of which is good for the bottom line and for investors."[147]

But as we saw earlier, just as in physics there is an antimatter for each matter, for each proponent of SRI investing there will be an opponent; opposing observers out there are bashing each other with different surveys, selective data points and personal opinions about ethical investing. On marketwatch.com, Derek Tharp writes that "some (SRI) strategies may have little or no impact, and each should be evaluated on its own merits. And because socially responsible strategies generally come with a higher cost to consumers, investors should carefully consider both the true costs and benefits of any given strategy."[148]

On theglobeandmail.com, David Berman goes one step further and writes: "The problem with SRI is that you limit your universe of stocks. And this limit simply cannot do a better job at building wealth." Towards the end of his article, Berman challenges the reader: "Have you found any ethical stocks or funds that outperform the market?"[149] I would like to take up that challenge – in fact it is not that hard to do. Over a 20-year period from 1998 to the first quarter of 2018, the Norwegian government pension fund that I mentioned earlier (SRI-managed) returned 4.0% in real terms after expenses and allowing for inflation.[150] The latest published 20-year real returns from the equivalent sovereign wealth fund in Singapore – GIC (no SRI policy) – are an annualised 3.7%.[151] Very similar, right? The Norwegians' ethical stance is not really detrimental to their overall returns; if anything it might help them marginally.

Let's look at more facts

To gauge your investment performance, you need a benchmark to compare it against. Let us say you have selected an ethical smart beta portfolio of stocks from the S&P 500 index; you would then calculate your total return from your portfolio and compare it with the results of your benchmark index over the same period. Likewise, when you consider an ethically managed SRI fund, check and see how this product compares with the broader market. The index provider MSCI has a broadly managed ESG index for Asia; let us see how it compared to the broader market as represented by the MSCI all-country Asia benchmark index over the last 10 years or so:

Asian ESG Shares versus Benchmark Index
(Rebased; Sep 2007 = 100)

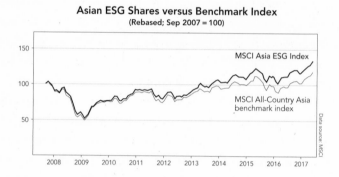

Not too bad, right? From the same index provider, the wider emerging market (EM) countries with and without an environmental, social and governance screen:

Emerging Markets ESG Shares versus Benchmark Index
(Rebased; Sep 2007 = 100)

Let us go even wider; here is the world index compared to the world SRI index:

World SRI Index versus World Index
(Rebased; Sep 2007 = 100)

We can also try a slightly different comparison over a longer period. $100 invested in the MSCI KLD Social 400 index in May 1990 would have grown to $1,426 by August 2017. This index provides exposure to companies with outstanding ESG ratings and excludes companies whose products have negative social or environmental impact. This compares favourably with the broader market index, the S&P 500; $100 invested here would have grown to "only" $1,334 over the same period.

KLD Social 400 Index versus S&P 500
(Rebased; May 1990 = 100)

Let us look at another case, the FTSE all-world share benchmark index compared to an index where fossil fuels are stripped out:

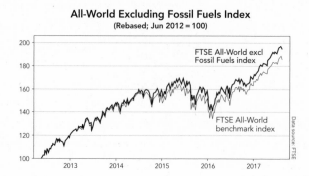

All-World Excluding Fossil Fuels Index
(Rebased; Jun 2012 = 100)

The conclusion is that stripping out the nasty fossil fuel companies would have rewarded investors during that period. Let us try something similar from the same data service provider, FTSE. The chart below shows four indexes tracking specific environmental sectors: water, energy efficiency, opportunities all-share and opportunities US. All four outperform the broader market all-cap benchmark index.

**FTSE Environmental Opportunities Indexes
versus Global All-Cap Benchmark**
(Rebased; Jun 2012 = 100)

MSCI and FTSE are among the leading index and financial data providers in the world; surely they cannot all be wrong? It seems to me that nice guys don't always finish last after all.

When I sift through all the noise out there surrounding ethical/SRI investing, my conclusion is that your SRI stance could make you money, or it could cost you money in some cases – as I showed earlier with the solar energy investment fiasco. But so could unethical/irresponsible investing, as we have also seen – remember the oil price collapse in 2014 and all the bankruptcies that followed? I can only conclude that at the end of the day it is your own personal strategy that is important. It is what makes you feel good that matters.

If it is any help to you, you might want to consider your investment strategy as a pyramid of priorities. Just like with any other portfolio, it helps to have a solid foundation of financially sound companies; depending on your risk appetite you can then build up from there and add a top layer of more risky small-cap stocks, which you hope might grow big and provide above-average returns one day. With regard to ethical investing, it seems to me that a similar strategy would work: Keep most of your hard-earned money safe in profitable companies that do not do too much harm – that is the broad ESG investing foundation. It is easy to find an ETF that screens out undesirable companies and as we saw above this is likely to improve, not diminish, your returns. Nowadays ETF expense ratios can be as low as 0.2–0.3% p.a. or even lower; so just buy and hold a product like that for the long term and feel good about it. If you are really dedicated, and have the time and inclination, by all means go into core SRI; build your own ethical fund by positively selecting the businesses you really like. Your risk will increase somewhat but should still be manageable if you diversify your portfolio of large- and medium-cap listed companies. Only then go into the risky ethical impact investing with a small portion of your funds; help out small-cap or unlisted start-ups you

Pyramid of Priorities

like and believe in, the organisations doing social or environmental good. Just be prepared to pay a price for your convictions.

So, regarding capital allocation, balancing and selection of companies, I can only tell you what I did, I cannot tell you what you should do. That is entirely up to you. Just remember that if you do consider yourself an ethical person, there are many different ways you can express that in your financial choices. Alternatively, you can just participate in the lucrative extractive industries "on the way down", as Naomi Klein says, but control your spending meanwhile; and when you can afford it, give back to nature. We will look at that in the next chapter.

10

Support the Supporters

*"Successful people have a social responsibility
to make the world a better place and
not just take from it."*

— CARRIE UNDERWOOD

The time is right

It is nice when celebrities such as young country singer Carrie Underwood make statements like that. It is true for all people – that each one of us has a responsibility to make this a better place – but it is especially true for people with the extra influence that fame and fortune have given them.

And the time to make a difference has never been better. First of all, we cannot pretend that we don't know what is going on; the data is out there for all to see, the facts are staring us in the face. With Google and Wikipedia and hundreds of other such sites available to billions of people, there is no place any longer for anyone to hide behind prejudice and unsubstantiated barricades of mistaken beliefs and wishful thinking. All data can easily be checked; we can choose to ignore it, but we cannot deny it. We know that the world is heading for ecological, economic and social disaster.

Professor Paul Ehrlich with Stanford University has been speaking out about humanity's unsustainable ways since the 1960s and he is losing patience with our inability to change. He says in an interview in 2018: "A shattering collapse of civilisation is a near certainty in the next few decades due to humanity's continuing destruction of the natural world." Ehrlich sees overpopulation, overconsumption and increasing toxification of the environment as existential dangers to all of us: "Population growth, along with over-consumption per capita, is driving civilisation over the edge: billions of people are now hungry or micronutrient-malnourished, and climate disruption is killing people." Ehrlich says that the world's optimum population is less than 2 billion people and that an unprecedented redistribution of wealth is needed to end the overconsumption of resources. But: "The rich who now run the global system – that hold the annual 'world destroyer' meetings in Davos – are unlikely to let it happen."[152]

The "meetings in Davos" remark refers to the World Economic Forum's annual gatherings in Switzerland; some 2,500 top economists, business executives and heads of state assemble at this ski resort to discuss the economic and political issues of the day. I agree with Ehrlich on many things, but calling these people "world destroyers" is perhaps a bit over the top. I will get back to this in a minute.

But secondly: the old ways of doing things are obviously not working. We cannot fix the economy by getting back to growth when growth itself is the problem. We cannot produce our way out of an economic situation caused by oversupply. We tell each other that if we all just look on the bright side, somehow everything will be fine. It will not. Anthropologist Jason Hickel wrote in the *Guardian* in 2015: "Growth isn't an option anymore – we've already grown too much. Since 1980, the global economy has grown by 380%, but the number of people living in poverty on less than $5 (£3.20) a day has increased by more than 1.1 billion. So much for the trickle-down effect." Dr Hickel believes it is time for the rich countries to consume less and accept a higher quality of life with less material stuff: "We need to reorient ourselves toward a positive future, a truer form of progress. One that is geared toward quality instead of quantity. One that is more sophisticated than just accumulating ever increasing amounts of stuff, which doesn't make anyone happier anyway. What is certain is that GDP as a measure is not going to get us there and we need to get rid of it." Hickel concludes that we don't really have a choice: "Either we slow down voluntarily or climate change will do it for us. We can't go on ignoring the laws of nature… If we do not act soon, all our hard-won gains against poverty will evaporate, as food systems collapse and mass famine re-emerges to an extent not seen since the 19th century."[153]

From a financial perspective, I would like to add that we have avoided facing reality for 10 years by expanding financial debt to astronomical levels. We don't know how this will end, simply because we have never had nearly as much debt before, but it is unlikely to end well.

And then finally, the third reason that this is a perfect time to help out: internet connectivity and the associated social media platforms available. Starting a Facebook page, a Twitter account or even a YouTube channel has never been easier. In *Postcapitalism* (2015), Paul Mason says: "The thing that is corroding capitalism, barely rationalised by mainstream economists, is information." Like many others, Mason works to find a better way forward; he feels that the current capitalist market system has failed us. I don't agree with all of Mason's viewpoints, but I do believe that unlimited access to information is a good thing, and that the new interactive digital media will make it easier for us to share ideas and progress.

Governmental versus non-governmental

It was the British actor Peter Ustinov who said back in the 1990s (quoted from memory): "I have never been stopped on the street

THE ETHICAL INVESTOR'S HANDBOOK

by someone collecting to buy more fighter jets and nuclear weapons. The governments always make sure we have plenty of that kind of stuff." I can see what Ustinov is saying: He would like governments to spend less on arms and more on welfare. In general, I think most people would agree with that. But you can also turn the quote around and conclude: It is nice when governments make an effort to protect the environment and social cohesion – but don't depend on it. Be prepared to engage with the non-governmental sector and private charities; they are the ones you see collecting on street corners to fight poverty and environmental decay.

Getting back to the Davos crowd that Ehrlich was picking on above: Yes, I cannot rule out that there are bad apples in the business elite – executives who don't care if they wreck the earth as long as they get rich. If you are anything like me, it will make you sick when you read in the papers about people who get arrested for fraud and corruption, and it turns out that they have squandered all their ill-gotten gains the nouveau riche way on expensive cars, watches and designer handbags. Sure, those people are out there.

But by and large, it is my observation that most wealthy people actually want to do what is right for themselves and their families, as well as society at large; they are not usually out to be "world destroyers", to use Ehrlich's words. My son Daniel puts it this way: "The stereotypical cultural image of the modern businessman and investor paints a very cynical picture of these workers as greedy and close-minded, but I think a lot of business and money people are also interested in making money in sound and responsible ways, and in the legacy they leave to the future." It is nice when young millennials like Daniel (born 1988) have these nuanced views.

And these views are in fact substantiated by data. In Chapter 5, I mentioned Ted Turner, who donated $1 billion to the UN. Turner said on that occasion in a CNN interview: "There's a lot of people who are awash in money they don't know what to do with. It doesn't do you any good if you don't know what to do with it. I have learned – the more good that I did, the more money comes in. You have to learn to give. You're not born as a giver. You're born selfish."[154] We need these rich people to step up and be a force for good, a counterweight to the Koch brothers, Rupert Murdoch and other not-so-ethical tycoons who lobby for more fossil fuel subsidies and defence spending through misinformation campaigns, with little regard for the consequences.

So following Turner's commitment, a lot of wealthy Americans such as Warren Buffett and Bill Gates have pledged to give most of their fortunes away when they are through with them. Those two tycoons started the Giving Pledge movement in 2010; others have joined in since then. The pledge is that participants commit to give away half or more of their wealth within their lifetime or in their will. The list of participants is an amazing collection of successful and generous private individuals and couples.

If I have a slight problem with all that personally, it is that whenever I check all these new charitable foundations, the money is inevitably given to people who help other people. Moguls like Buffett and Gates who got rich selling consumer products and computer software naturally want to give back to their customers – I get that. They probably would like to have more customers and more people in general. But I think this is wrong. Bill Gates, who genuinely likes to help others, should divert some of his considerable resources, not to encourage having more people on Earth, but fewer. It is the only humane thing to do. What we do need – with the earth on the brink of collapse – is more natural capital, more wilderness areas, more biodiversity. So if you can spare any money, give it to people who work for nature. The Turner Foundation does that.

People should help themselves; we shouldn't rely on the rich or elected governments to bail us out. In each society there will be some people – typically 10–12% of the population – who for some reason or other make bad life choices. We have those here in Singapore as well. The authorities watch their utilities accounts; when they cannot pay for their power, those households are usually in real trouble. Divorced single mothers, pathological gamblers, alcoholic old men with no family... that sort of people, you find those in all countries. You have to help them, without inadvertently subsidising or encouraging their way of life; it is a difficult choice, but in Singapore I think we get the balance right. The other 90% of the population can and should help themselves through life's ups and downs. That is part of the challenge – you learn from the bad times as well as from the good. If you don't like where you are at, fine; just don't get into a boat and barge into another country unlawfully. Go down to the embassy and apply for a residence permit the legitimate way. In Singapore we don't accept illegal immigrants, but we do provide work for some 1.3 million people from abroad who get a chance to come here and better themselves; it is an astonishingly efficient system that has worked great for so many, myself included!

Finding solutions

So if you can, help those who help our earth. Animals and rainforests and coral reefs cannot help themselves; we humans have to fix this. There are thousands of enthusiastic young (and not so young) people lining up to help, but they need resources. For a short period while living in Denmark from 1994 to 1996, I worked for the Danish ornithological society DOF/BirdLife as their international officer. Officially it was a job, but in reality I worked 30+ hours a week for DKK10,500 per month; after taxes my take-home pay was less than DKK5,000 per month (US$780) – with three small kids to support at the time, this would not have worked had I not had some additional passive investment income. I don't really believe in volunteering; volunteers too often take work away from real workers who depend on that work – such as guiding eco-tourists or doing wildlife surveys or collecting garbage – for income. But I do believe in being financially free, and then joining others working for very little, while doing the right thing!

Anyway, one of my tasks with BirdLife International was raising funds for our conservation projects; that meant knocking on countless doors among government agencies and private donors for contributions. It was an interesting learning process, but one of the things I found was that donors love to give money to stuff: project vehicles, travel expenses, buildings, purchase of land, that sort of thing. They frowned when we asked for money to pay staff salaries. Yet I believe that is the best way you can help nature: pay people to go out there and do studies, file reports, work with local communities, patrol protected areas – we need people for all that.

One of the new catchphrases in philanthropy is "venture philanthropy", i.e. a crossover between pure philanthropy and impact investing. Nature conservation projects provide ample opportunities for that sort of arrangements. You need to be on the right side of history; taking care of the earth will be the great challenge of the future and we need all hands on deck.

Just be aware of some of the pitfalls out there, even in the nature do-gooder space. Not all the proposals brought forward are a good idea. I mentioned the CCS issue earlier – Carbon Capture and Storage – something like this is bound to come up again once in a while, but is unlikely to work. Some projects like that do more harm than good. In *This Changes Everything*, Naomi Klein deals with some of these proposals to provide technological fixes to environmental problems and she takes most of them to task. But this issue is hard to bury for good. In 2018, *Today Online* could report on a project to "step up research into dimming sunshine to curb climate change, hoping to judge if a man-made chemical sunshade would be less risky than a harmful rise in global temperatures. However, the report also mentioned that "a United Nations panel of climate experts, in a leaked draft of a report about global warming due for publication in October (2018), is skeptical about solar geo-engineering, saying it may be 'economically, socially and institutionally infeasible'. Among risks, the draft obtained by Reuters says it might disrupt weather patterns, could be hard to stop once started, and might discourage countries from making a promised switch from fossil fuels to cleaner energies."[155] So it seems to be "back to the drawing board" for those philanthropists.

One of the in-things in the do-gooder world is "carbon offset". As you might know, the airline industry is one of the big consumers of petroleum – in the form of jet fuel – and as such it contributes 1.3% a year to global man-made carbon emissions. That fuel consumption is estimated to grow somewhere between 2.8 and 3.9 times by 2040, compared to 2010 levels.[156] The source for that statement is a *Straits Times* report from 2016, which said: "A historic United Nations consensus to cap carbon emissions for the aviation sector has received solid backing from major countries. The scheme calls for voluntary participation from 2021; it will become compulsory in 2027 for most countries." So while the industry will continue to expand their fuel consumption, the airlines participating in the so-called Montreal agreement "will have to offset or neutralise excess carbon dioxide emissions, likely by investing in projects to reduce carbon emissions. Airlines are expected to spend more than US$25 billion to buy credits in 2035, or about 1 percent of projected total revenue."

But here is the thing about carbon offset: It doesn't really work, and in the worst-case scenario it could act as a green light for big polluters to just pay a bit of tax – a symbolic 1% in this case, passed on to consumers – and otherwise go on with business as usual. Don't take my word for it. In *How To Go Carbon Neutral*, do-gooder Mark Brassington writes: "Off-setting is just an example of 'green-washing', i.e corporate propaganda." And later in the book: "This practice of 'off-setting' is especially dangerous because it encourages people to think that it is actually carbon neutral, when it isn't."

One of the carbon offsetting mechanisms used by big polluters is the REDD programme – Reducing Emissions from Deforestation and Degradation. Sounds great, right? Polluters in the First World pay poor people in developing countries with a lot of forest and biodiversity not to cut their trees. A kind of environmental black-mail, if you will – countries like Indonesia and Vietnam saying to rich countries like Norway and Denmark: Give us some money or we will destroy our home.

But does it work? In 2017, the Danish daily *Jyllandsposten* reported that a Danish social scientist Thorkil Casse with Roskilde University travelled to REDD project sites in Vietnam and Indonesia to see what happened to the 400 million Danish kroners (about $62 million) that the Danish government had provided since 2009 for forest conservation under the REDD programme. When Dr Casse first arrived in Vietnam's Lam Dong province, the project initially looked promising. There was a nice new building for the local REDD office in the city of Dalat with some 15 people working to shuffle paper around and do reporting. But when Casse asked to see the forest, he realised that nothing was happening on location; not one of the many millions of dollars had reached the local population; instead the land had been divided between various industries. "I started seeing through the smoke screen that had been put out with the nice office and the many employees; it was just a stage, because there was nothing going on behind it – nothing was going on at the local level" – Casse told the paper. He found the same thing when he visited the Danish project site in Indonesia: "In those areas where the local population was sup-posed to be paid not to cut the forest, they had no control over the land. The land had been divided up by the authorities and awarded to companies doing mining, logging and palm oil production." Casse concluded in the report: "For the countries signing up to the REDD programme it is all about reputation. So they sign on, but continue business as usual." The report summarised the result this way: "The billion-dollar REDD project by the UN and World Bank is a fiasco."[157]

Since 2015, the United Nations has also been instrumental in developing a set of so-called Sustainable Development Goals (SDGs) as part of the 2030 Agenda for Sustainable Development. Kudos to the UN for doing this.[158] The 17 goals are, as you would expect, all very noble; however, neutral observers have pointed out that many of them contradict each other: Goal 8 (economic growth) and 9 (infrastructure) will be difficult to implement in harmony with others such as 11 (sustainability) and 13 (climate action). Increasing wages and reducing cost of living might be difficult to do at the same time. There are no specific targets and also no real mechanisms in place anyway for achieving any of this – that is up to the member countries.

Therefore it should come as no surprise when a subsequent UN report in 2018 concluded: "The Asia Pacific region is failing to meet almost two-thirds of the targets set by the United Nations Sustainable Development Goals (SDGs), with no progress seen in efforts to protect the oceans and forests, reduce inequality or take action on climate change. Besides environmental targets, efforts to promote decent work and inclusive economic growth (Goal 8), to reduce inequality (Goal 10), and to build justice, peace and strong institutions (Goal 16) have had limited success or shown regression as rapid economic growth has not been equitably shared. Targets focusing on environmental sustainability for life below water (Goal 14) and life on land (Goal 15) show no improvement. Since 2015, the health of the region's oceans has declined as more plastic than ever is finding its way into waterways. Life below water continues to be depleted without strong measures to conserve marine resources while Asian countries remain the world's top five plastic polluters. Asia's performance in safeguarding life on land (Goal 15) is faring no better. Since 2015, protection of conserved forests and other natural resources has weakened. Fragmentation of habitats due to deforestation and environmental degradation from extractive industries continue unabated."[159]

A simpler way

Nevertheless, in spite of all the setbacks and failures, I still maintain that this is an exciting time for everyone working to save the earth. Every day new data comes in that we have to process and consider. Thousands – if not millions – of people see the risks and engage themselves in finding solutions. My wife just bought herself a re-usable stainless steel drinking straw that she carries around with her to cut down on our consumption of plastic. Saving the earth one straw at a time!

I mentioned in Chapter 1 that within my short lifetime, biodiversity and wilderness areas have crashed. But that doesn't mean that there is no nature left for the next generation. The baseline has simply just shifted down a lot; but if half the world's coral reefs are gone due to bleaching and dynamite fishing, well, there is still another half left! We have to guard and appreciate that half, and all the rest of nature that is left. "Rewilding" is the new key phrase in nature conservation circles; there is heaps of work to be done for future ecologists protecting and restoring what is left.

As we have seen, the sustainability movement is fraught with contradictions and dead-ends. But that shouldn't stop us from trying to find better solutions. The question is not "Can we afford to save the earth?"; the question is "Can we afford not to?". Already the famous *Stern Review* that came out in 2006 concluded: "Using the results from formal economic models, the Review estimates that if we don't act, the overall costs and risks of climate change will be equivalent to losing at least 5% of global GDP each year, now and forever. If a wider range of risks and impacts is taken into account, the estimates of damage could rise to 20% of GDP or more. In contrast, the costs of action – reducing greenhouse gas emissions to avoid the worst impacts of climate change – can be limited to around 1% of global GDP each year."[160] The choices should really be quite obvious; there are more details in the 662-page review that is easy to find online.

During my brief stint as a junior corporate executive with Core Laboratories Ltd in the 1980s, I was sent on a time-management training seminar by my company. I don't remember much from it, but I did learn one vital thing: The tasks in front of you can be divided into two categories: the urgent and the important. Don't get too caught up with all the urgent matters only. Pay attention to the important ones as well, before they also become urgent! Fixing our environmental Ponzi scheme doesn't appear very urgent at the moment; but it is important, and we should put it right now before it also becomes urgent.

So it will be expensive if we don't act now and reduce our environmental footprint; but as I have made clear, personally I don't see any signs that we will, not in a meaningful and effective manner anyway. The *Stern Review* also concluded that: "All countries will be affected by climate change, but the poorest countries will suffer earliest and most."[161] With ecological collapse comes economic hardship, depressed asset prices and eventually social disintegration. Hurricane Katrina in New Orleans in 2005 showed us that even a well-organised society like the US can fairly easily come unglued under environmental stress.

So what to do? Each one of us will have to find our own way forward. Like I mentioned, I cannot tell you what you should do. I can only tell you that over time I have come to believe that our best way forward is basically a more simple life, with less stuff and less clutter and less stress. And I am not the only one who thinks this way. Check out this excellent little site and see if it inspires you: simplerway.org.

The Simpler Way

Personally I am always a bit sceptical of "holier than thou" groups that claim to have seen the light, and now everyone has to follow. But that doesn't mean that you cannot selectively pick some value from people who think outside the box. The Simpler Way philosophy makes a lot of sense to me, considering the situation we are in now where more production and more construction and more material stuff don't really seem to be making us much happier. Here is how the Simpler Way movement's website describes their philosophy:

"By now we all understand the importance of reducing resource and energy consumption and stepping more lightly on the planet. But figuring out exactly how to do this in a consumer society can be very challenging. The Simpler Way represents a life with less clutter, less waste, and less fossil fuel use, but also a life with more time for the things that truly inspire and bring happiness.

"Too many people today spend their entire lives desperately climbing the endless ladder of consumerism, seeking more and more income to spend on more and more stuff. But at the end of life these people inevitably discover that they have not really lived, that they have wasted their only chance at life inside a shopping mall. A free and meaningful life, it turns out, does not actually depend on having all the latest consumer products or having the nicest house on the street. On the contrary, working long hours just to 'keep up with the Joneses' leaves people with less time for the things that really matter in life, like friends, family, community, and engaging in peaceful, creative activity."

The Simpler Way suggests a number of concrete ways to escape the materialistic rut:
- Get out of debt and rethink your spending; budget and start saving.
- Downsize your home and/or share with family and friends.
- Avoid long commutes; bike to work if you can or work from home.
- Eat healthily; grow and cook your own food if you can.
- Buy second-hand clothes or swap with friends.
- Share tools and skills with family and friends.
- Reduce consumption in general, especially of energy and water.
- Avoid buying cheap, unjustly manufactured goods.
- Keep technology simple and lasting.
- Adopt a mindful attitude to life; ask yourself: How much is "enough"?

Everyone can pitch in

Ethical investing could be a part of this simpler and more pleasant life. I recommend it because I think you will do better and be happier and wealthier that way. The practice is still in its infancy, but as we saw in Chapter 5, the trend is growing; globally the assets under SRI strategy management account for about 25% of the total, and Asia is catching up to that number fast. A survey conducted by Standard Chartered Private Bank in 2018 found that wealthy investors in Singapore, Hong Kong, China and India are looking to increase their share of SRI investments to overall 19%. The report also found that even among these high-net-worth individuals more education is needed: "Despite 86 per cent of investors claiming to be currently engaged in sustainable investing, there is a significant knowledge gap among the respondents around what sustainable investing entails, as well as the returns and impact it can deliver."[162]

Specifically relating to Singapore, Jacqueline Teo wrote in an op-ed on *Eco-business* that there is still room for improvement among local investors: "While global movements such as the Principles for Responsible Investment (PRI) and Equator Principles are increasing awareness about green investments, giving rise to a small but growing number of specialised green funds, such shifts in investor behaviour are not seen in Singapore. The challenge for Singapore is not the lack of awareness, but the difficulty of translating awareness to action. Educational campaigns aimed at empowering not only investors, but also citizens, to act upon their climate change concerns may be more effective in nudging companies and financial institutions to embrace sustainability."[163]

Although ethical investing should be part of your strategy, I believe that times will be tough going forward. As an investor, it will be difficult to achieve the same return on capital that we have enjoyed for the past 10 years or so since the financial crisis and the Great Recession. The mountain of debt that we have generated in recent years will have to be addressed one way or other. This unwinding of liabilities will hurt return on capital and might even cause a scenario of falling asset prices.

On top of that there is the issue of declining productivity. Due to the enormous expansion of cheap labour that happened after China opened up and the Soviet Union and its satellite states entered the market economy in the early 1990s, production has increased, but productivity – overall output per working hour – has increased very little, if at all. In an era where we are moving towards a more circular – so-called weightless – economy, where most information and many service functions are increasingly free, conventional productivity cannot increase much. As a case in point, imagine what free Skype calls have cost the big telecom companies. Conventional financial services might be in for a similar shake-up soon, with free advice, money transfers and peer-to-peer lending gaining ground fast. The new darlings of the stock markets such as Amazon and Alibaba operate on razor-thin margins and are taking market share from the traditionally high-value-added retail sector. We don't even know what an era of robotics and artificial intelligence will entail, should that ever happen.

Therefore I agree with economist Lee Su Shyan when she writes for the *Straits Times* that the days of high economic growth and return on capital for investors are behind us. Apart from other reasons, Lee also mentions an ageing population and increasing levels of taxation as factors that will dampen incomes and prosperity going forward. Older people generally make less money and spend less, while governments everywhere have to increase taxes to cover debts and/or increasingly generous welfare and defence expenditures. In this world, only Russia is reducing their defence spending year over year; every other country I can think of is increasing theirs. Lee concludes, referring to the global stagnation: "The outlook for (low) returns in the Singapore market is likely to be similar. People will have to work longer to save more just to maintain the same level of return."[164]

As I have repeatedly stated, in spite of all my reservations about our environmental predicaments and our fragile economic situation in general, I think that savers should be invested in the stock market, preferably in an ethical and long-term manner. The markets are a reflection of our whole social state of affairs, and you just have to be involved. Life is not a spectator sport. Not doing anything is also a way of acting.

As for the Singapore stock market, right now (May 2018), the Price/Earnings ratio for the SPDR ETF tracking the Straits Times Index is about 11.6; the historical ratio is 16.9. So is this a reasonable level? I should think so; the American market is much higher: the S&P 500, for comparison, is trading at around 25 PE. Can the market go lower from here? Of course it can, much lower; it has dropped as low as 6 times earnings during the bottom in March 2009.[165] Check your own local stock market and see if you are comfortable with the levels; if you are, then invest in some companies you like.

And try to be an ethical investor if you can. By that I mean someone who wants to generate a return on capital without wrecking the earth. You will feel better that way, and with a bit of effort you will also do better. So to sum up, here is a strategy that I recommend for the ethical worker, saver and investor. This strategy has worked for me:

1. If you must, to get ahead, work for a while in the extractive economy.

2. While you do that, control your spending, keep your consumption down and generate wealth; be a "financial doomsday prepper".

3. Invest your savings to generate passive income, without necessarily ruining the earth.

4. When financially free, support those who support the environment, and pitch in yourself if you possibly can.

Notes

1. http://mm.aftenposten.no/kloden-var/?artikkel=den-tause-vaaren-i-fuglefjellet
2. https://www.dr.dk/ligetil/tre-millioner-fugle-er-forsvundet-i-danmark
3. https://jyllands-posten.dk/international/europa/ECE10443392/pesticider-skyld-i-massiv-fugledoed-i-frankrig/
4. https://newsbreak.dk/der-bliver-faerre-fugle-i-europa/
5. https://www.theguardian.com/environment/2015/aug/26/conservationists-appalled-at-illegal-killing-of-25m-birds-a-year-in-the-mediterranean
6. http://www.komitee.de/en/projects/germany
7. https://www.birdlife.org/asia/news/silencing-songbirds
8. http://www.endangeredearth.com/
9. https://www.theguardian.com/environment/2016/oct/19/worlds-mammals-being-eaten-into-extinction-report-warns
10. https://news.mongabay.com/2016/10/hunting-not-deforestation-biggest-threat-to-southeast-asian-biodiversity-study/
11. Seng, Lim K. 2009. The Avifauna of Singapore. Singapore: Nature Society (S)
12. https://www.independent.co.uk/travel/asia/bali-plastic-pollution-sea-diver-video-indonesia-problem-manta-rays-a8246241.html
13. http://www.bbc.com/news/science-environment-43477233
14. Davis, Neil. 1982. Alaska Science Nuggets. Fairbanks: University of Alaska
15. https://theconversation.com/after-25-years-of-trying-why-arent-we-environmentally-sustainable-yet-73911
16. https://19january2017snapshot.epa.gov/climate-impacts/climate-impacts-alaska_.html
17. http://www.todayonline.com/singapore/destruction-environment-overpopulation-top-risks-mankind-say-top-scientists
18. http://www.dw.com/en/slavery-in-the-21st-century/av-41611160

19. http://www.todayonline.com/world/
    why-china-must-wake-demographic-reality
20. http://www.todayonline.com/singapore/
    spores-demographic-time-bomb-starts-ticking-next-year-uob-report
21. https://www.borger.dk/familie-og-boern/familieydelser-oversigt/
    boerne-ungeydelse
22. https://blogs.wsj.com/chinarealtime/2013/04/18/
    heres-how-much-poverty-has-declined-in-china/
23. https://www.channelnewsasia.com/news/asiapacific/more-than-
    100-killed-since-philippine-police-returned-to-duterte-s-drug-
    war-10010026
24. http://science.time.com/2013/04/19/
    why-empowering-poor-women-is-good-for-the-planet/
25. https://www.populationmatters.org/goodall-population/
26. https://www.theguardian.com/environment/2017/jul/12/
    want-to-fight-climate-change-have-fewer-children
27. http://money.cnn.com/2016/05/10/news/economy/us-debt-ownership/
    index.html
28. https://finance.yahoo.com/blogs/just-explain-it/why-mortgage-rates-
    matter-152241574.html
29. http://www.eco-business.com/opinion/
    the-fed-has-accepted-climate-change-risk-whats-next/
30. https://www.reuters.com/article/ecb-policy-bonds/graphic-one-in-five-
    euro-bonds-yields-less-than-ecbs-deposit-rate-idUSL5N1ES1CJ
31. https://www.dbs.com.sg/personal/support/bank-deposit-accounts-fall-
    below-fee.html
32. https://www.singstat.gov.sg/statistics/visualising-data/charts/
    share-of-gdp-by-industry
33. https://www.bis.org/publ/otc_hy1711.htm
34. https://tradingeconomics.com/united-states/inflation-cpi
35. http://thefinance.sg/2017/09/03/be-a-financial-doomsday-prepper/
36. http://wwf.panda.org/about_our_earth/all_publications/lpr_2016/
37. http://theconversation.com/
    how-the-great-phosphorus-shortage-could-leave-us-all-hungry-54432
38. https://www.iea.org/weo2017/
39. https://www.bloomberg.com/news/articles/2017-10-30/
    singapore-is-finding-it-harder-to-grow-literally
40. http://www.redd-monitor.org/2016/03/03/norway-admits-that-we-
    havent-seen-actual-progress-in-reducing-deforestation-in-indonesia/
41. http://www.reuters.com/article/us-global-debt-iif-idUSKBN14O1PQ
42. https://www.nytimes.com/2014/06/05/science/earth/putting-a-price-
    tag-on-natures-defenses.html

43. https://www.sciencedaily.com/releases/2018/03/180323093734.htm
44. https://news.mongabay.com/2018/04/new-research-examines-spread-of-payments-for-ecosystem-services-around-the-globe/
45. Burgess, A. et al. (eds.). 2017. *Pocket World Figures*. London: Profile Books.
46. https://quoteinvestigator.com/2011/10/20/last-tree-cut/
47. https://theconversation.com/raja-ampat-why-reefs-are-worth-more-money-than-mines-2163
48. https://www.youtube.com/watch?v=DSlB1nW4S54
49. https://www.weforum.org/agenda/2017/06/there-are-now-more-refugees-than-the-entire-population-of-the-uk/
50. http://www.worldbank.org/en/news/press-release/2018/03/19/climate-change-could-force-over-140-million-to-migrate-within-countries-by-2050-world-bank-report
51. Geh Min. 2018. "Protect our environmental reserves like fiscal reserves." *The Straits Times*, 30 Jan.
52. https://www.reuters.com/article/us-venezuela-economy/venezuela-2016-inflation-hits-800-percent-gdp-shrinks-19-percent-document-idUSKBN154244
53. Lee, K.Y. (2000). *From Third World to First*. Times Media, Singapore.
54. https://iq-research.info/en/average-iq-by-country
55. http://worldhappiness.report/
56. https://www.todayonline.com/world/finland-worlds-happiest-country-us-discontent-grows-un-report
57. https://www.oecd.org/tax/revenue-statistics-denmark.pdf
58. https://knoema.com/atlas
59. https://www.dst.dk/da/Statistik/Publikationer/VisPub?cid=20752
60. https://www.police.gov.sg/news-and-publications/statistics
61. https://www.iras.gov.sg/irashome/Quick-Links/Tax-Rates/Individual-Income-Tax-Rates/
62. https://www.ussif.org/files/SIF_Trends_16_Executive_Summary(1).pdf
63. http://www.gsi-alliance.org/wp-content/uploads/2017/03/GSIR_Review2016.F.pdf
64. https://www.investopedia.com/university/ethical-investing/ethical-investing2.asp
65. https://az768132.vo.msecnd.net/documents/54768_2018_02_15_04_55_25_303.gzip.pdf
66. https://www.reuters.com/article/us-environment-barrier-reef-funding/australia-announces-379-million-funding-for-great-barrier-reef-idUSKBN1I0036
67. https://www.worldsmostethicalcompanies.com/honorees/country/united-states/

68. https://www.hrc.org/resources/best-places-to-work-2017
69. http://www.straitstimes.com/business/companies-markets/3-spore-companies-among-worlds-most-sustainable-firms
70. http://www.corporateknights.com/reports/2018-global-100/2018-global-100-results-15166618/
71. https://www.zmescience.com/science/nestle-company-pollution-children/
72. http://sustainablebusinessawards.com/enter/
73. http://www.straitstimes.com/singapore/environment/ntuc-fairprice-sheng-siong-prime-supermarket-remove-all-asia-pulp-paper-group
74. https://www.nytimes.com/2016/12/03/business/energy-environment/how-big-banks-are-putting-rain-forests-in-peril.html
75. https://www.regnskog.no/en/news/new-report-calls-out-nordic-countries-commitment-to-forest-protection-by-linking-nordic-banks-and-government-pension-funds-to-indonesias-palm-oil-deforestation.
76. http://www.autoguide.com/auto-news/2016/03/tesla-model-s-categorized-as-a-high-polluter-in-singapore.html
77. http://www.autoguide.com/auto-news/2016/04/would-you-believe-a-tesla-model-s-causes-more-pollution-than-a-bmw-3-series-.html
78. https://www.nbcnews.com/mach/science/stephen-hawking-says-humans-must-leave-earth-within-600-years-ncna818926
79. http://www.bbc.com/news/world-us-canada-43860590.
80. http://www.newindianexpress.com/business/press-releases/2018/feb/15/controversial-economist-predicts-that-india-could-dethrone-western-wealth-and-power-1773770.html
81. https://energiwatch.dk/article10474731.ece
82. https://politiken.dk/debat/debatindlaeg/art6508380/Politikerne-spiller-hasard-med-vores-fremtid
83. http://epublications.bond.edu.au/cgi/viewcontent.cgi?article=1075&context=cm
84. https://genius.com/Johnny-cash-man-in-black-lyrics
85. https://www.valuepenguin.sg/best-online-brokerages-singapore#nogo
86. https://www.wsj.com/video/gmo-grantham-stocks-decently-different-this-time/D98E2C49-45CC-4F63-B304-7B6C5D26C7C8.html
87. http://money.cnn.com/2018/03/25/news/companies/remington-bankruptcy/index.html
88. http://www.scmp.com/business/companies/article/2140784/ubs-introduces-first-pure-green-investment-portfolio-asia
89. https://uk.reuters.com/article/us-emerging-bonds-green/emerging-climate-bonds-boom-but-are-they-really-green-idUKKCN1AY1F4
90. http://www.eco-business.com/news/will-a-lack-of-transparency-hurt-green-bonds/

91. https://www.dbs.com/annualreports/2013/annexure-statistics.html
92. https://www.gic.com.sg/about-gic/sustainability/
93. http://etikkradet.no/files/2017/04/Etikkraadet_Guidelines-_eng_2017_web.pdf
94. https://www.nbim.no/en/responsibility/exclusion-of-companies/
95. http://earthguide.ucsd.edu/virtualmuseum/climatechange2/07_1.shtml
96. https://qz.com/1045619/germanys-diesel-scandal-shines-a-light-on-how-indulgent-the-government-is-with-carmakers/
97. https://www.theverge.com/2017/7/24/16021292/german-car-companies-cartel-diesel-emissions-90s
98. http://fortune.com/2018/02/06/volkswagen-vw-emissions-scandal-penalties/
99. https://jyllands-posten.dk/debat/breve/ECE10579291/folkebevaegelsens-store-miljoebluff/
100. https://uk.reuters.com/article/aker-carbon/aker-says-may-pull-plug-on-carbon-capture-project-idUKL6E7M40K320111104
101. https://www.motherjones.com/politics/2014/02/study-weve-been-underestimating-methane-leaks-natural-gas-plants-years/
102. https://www.channelnewsasia.com/news/cnainsider/lng-natural-gas-electricity-singapore-energy-security-tank-10088910
103. https://www.economist.com/news/business/21702493-natural-gass-reputation-cleaner-fuel-coal-and-oil-risks-being-sullied-methane
104. http://www.powerengineeringint.com/articles/2018/01/disruption-expert-says-by-2025-every-new-vehicle-will-be-electric.html
105. https://www.theguardian.com/world/2018/jan/18/norway-aims-for-all-short-haul-flights-to-be-100-electric-by-2040
106. https://www.lta.gov.sg/content/ltaweb/en/roads-and-motoring/transport-options-for-motorists/encouraging-green-vehicles/Promoting-Clean-and-Energy-Efficient-Vehicles.html
107. http://www.straitstimes.com/singapore/environment/solar-power-capacity-soars-in-singapore
108. https://www.stocksbnb.com/reports/phillip-2018-singapore-strategy-utilities/
109. https://theconversation.com/the-state-of-the-us-solar-industry-5-questions-answered-90578
110. https://www.greentechmedia.com/articles/read/rest-in-peace-the-list-of-deceased-solar-companies#gs.I4Q3p5o
111. https://windeurope.org/wp-content/uploads/files/about-wind/statistics/WindEurope-Annual-Statistics-2017.pdf
112. https://www.bloomberg.com/gadfly/articles/2018-03-28/we-all-love-wind-power-unless-you-want-to-make-money

113. http://www.davidjkent-writer.com/2017/05/08/nikola-tesla-and-the-development-of-hydroelectric-power-at-niagara-falls/
114. https://www.statista.com/statistics/643369/electricity-prices-for-households-in-norway/
115. https://www.straitstimes.com/asia/se-asia/malaysia-tribes-say-controversial-borneo-dam-is-scrapped
116. http://www.guinnessworldrecords.com/world-records/highest-score-by-the-environmental-sustainability-index-(country)
117. https://www.doe.gov.ph/philippine-power-statistics
118. https://www.geothermal-energy.org/
119. http://blogs.discovermagazine.com/crux/2016/03/23/nuclear-fusion-reactor-research/#.WvFOCKSFPcc
120. https://www.cnbc.com/2017/05/26/elon-musk-hates-hydrogen-but-automakers-are-still-investing-in-it.html
121. https://www.ft.com/content/b7caeae2-3888-3f2a-900e-c9bc8402599b
122. https://www.todayonline.com/voices/shared-bikes-are-looking-be-form-wastage#cxrecs_s
123. https://www.todayonline.com/commentary/curing-ills-shared-economy
124. https://www.todayonline.com/commentary/are-we-era-uneconomic-growth
125. https://jyllands-posten.dk/nyviden/ECE10587555/turisme-er-en-kaempe-klimasynder/
126. https://drmu.wordpress.com/2010/04/17/tourism-strategy/
127. http://www.bbc.com/news/world-43700833
128. https://earthchildjordykm.wordpress.com/2012/08/26/saving-one-species-and-losing-three/
129. https://www.accuweather.com/en/weather-news/michigan-confirms-nestle-water-extraction-sparking-public-outrage/70004797
130. https://news.nationalgeographic.com/2018/02/cape-town-running-out-of-water-drought-taps-shutoff-other-cities/
131. https://www.todayonline.com/world/warming-water-crisis-then-unrest-how-iran-fits-alarming-pattern
132. https://www.theedgesingapore.com/5-listed-environmental-plays-watch-china-goes-green
133. https://www.slideshare.net/DeminDamianWang/american-birding-association-digital-marketing-analysis-report?qid=2e7f60ef-9c98-4ce3-ac39-d0107c4c9176&v=&b=&from_search=1
134. https://www.atmos-chem-phys.net/8/389/2008/
135. http://www.gem.sciences-po.fr/content/research_topics/trade/ebp_pdf/GSI-European_Report_on_support_to_Biofuels-oct07.pdf

136. https://www.reuters.com/article/us-eu-biodiesel-analysis/europe-struggles-to-stem-biodiesel-import-flood-idUSKCN1GJ2I9
137. http://science.sciencemag.org/content/319/5867/1235
138. http://www.eco-business.com/news/debate-follows-british-supermarket-chains-decision-to-ban-palm-oil/
139. http://www.earthsave.org/environment.htm
140. https://jyllands-posten.dk/nyviden/ECE10670115/nye-tal-saa-meget-ville-det-gavne-jorden-hvis-vi-spiste-mindre-koed/
141. https://www.nytimes.com/2012/03/13/health/research/red-meat-linked-to-cancer-and-heart-disease.html
142. http://www.eco-business.com/news/the-fight-over-meatless-meat-is-starting-to-bite/
143. Strange, Morten. 2016. *Be Financially Free*. Singapore: Marshall Cavendish.
144. https://www.todayonline.com/singapore/smart-people-are-not-always-best-investors
145. https://www.cfapubs.org/toc/rf/2014/2014/1
146. http://www.exposingtruth.com/new-un-report-finds-almost-no-industry-profitable-if-environmental-costs-were-included/#ixzz464mYxl1L
147. https://www.todayonline.com/singapore/investing-make-social-impact
148. https://www.marketwatch.com/story/the-big-snag-in-ethical-investing-2017-09-14
149. https://www.theglobeandmail.com/globe-investor/investor-community/trading-shots/ethical-investing-a-feel-good-way-to-lose-money/article5043743/
150. https://www.nbim.no/en/the-fund/return-on-the-fund/
151. https://www.straitstimes.com/business/economy/gic-posts-steady-real-returns-of-37-amid-uncertainty
152. https://www.theguardian.com/cities/2018/mar/22/collapse-civilisation-near-certain-decades-population-bomb-paul-ehrlich
153. https://www.theguardian.com/global-development-professionals-network/2015/sep/23/developing-poor-countries-de-develop-rich-countries-sdgs
154. https://www.nytimes.com/1997/09/19/world/ted-turner-plans-a-1-billion-gift-for-un-agencies.html
155. https://www.todayonline.com/world/developing-nations-study-ways-dim-sunshine-slow-warming
156. Kaur, Karamjit. 2016. "Aviation emission control scheme gets solid backing." *The Straits Times*, 8 October.
157. http://jyllands-posten.dk/nyviden/ECE9437098/efter-ni-aar-regnskovsprojekt-til-milliarder-har-intet-aendret/

158. https://sustainabledevelopment.un.org/content/
     documents/4538pressowg13.pdf
159. http://www.eco-business.com/news/
     asia-pacific-falling-behind-on-two-thirds-of-sdg-targets/
160. http://mudancasclimaticas.cptec.inpe.br/~rmclima/pdfs/destaques/
     sternreview_report_complete.pdf
161. https://www.theguardian.com/politics/2006/oct/30/economy.uk
162. https://www.sc.com/en/media/press-release/
     sustainable-investments-on-the-rise-in-asia/
163. http://www.eco-business.com/opinion/
     singapore-not-yet-a-rising-green-finance-hub/
164. Lee, Su Shyan. 2016. "The hunt for good investment yields." *The Straits
     Times,* 28 September.
165. https://sg.finance.yahoo.com/news/singapore-stock-market-cheap-
     expensive-040426435.html

Glossary

Aggregate: The collective whole formed by several different parts. Aggregate demand is all the demand across the whole of the economy.

AGM: Annual general meeting.

Bloomberg Television: An American 24-hour financial cable TV channel reaching more than 300 million homes worldwide.

Cap: Used in finance as short for "capitalisation", i.e. share price times number of shares, the market value of the company.

CCS: Carbon Capture and Storage; the process of isolating and reinjecting CO_2 into the ground; a technique which is – and probably always will be – in the experimental phase.

CEO: Chief Executive Officer; the most senior executive in a private corporation; he or she reports to the board of directors.

CNBC: An American 24-hour cable TV channel covering financial news; owned by NBCUniversal News Group.

CPF: Central Provident Fund; a compulsory social security savings scheme for Singaporean citizens and permanent residents.

CPI: Consumer Price Index; a measure of inflation rates; core inflation is the CPI basket of consumer goods stripped of food and energy items (in Singapore, accommodation and private transport are also stripped out).

DBS: Formerly the Development Bank of Singapore; Singapore's largest government-linked retail bank.

Derivative: A financial instrument that derives its value from another – the underlying – asset, such as a futures contract or an option.

Dow Jones: Short for Dow Jones Industrial Average; an index tracking the performance of 30 major American corporations listed on the NYSE and NASDAQ.

DTM: Demographic Transition Model; a model in development economics that teaches that mature societies tend to have stabilising and eventually declining populations.

EM: Emerging markets; less-developed countries, some with rapid catch-up economic growth, such as China, India and Brazil.

EPA: The Environmental Protection Agency; an agency under the American federal government based in Washington, D.C., with a broad mandate to provide protection for the environment.

ESG: Environmental Social and Governance; the three main criteria applied for judging the ethical and sustainable status of a company.

ETF: Exchange-Traded Fund; a type of mutual fund that tracks an index or asset class, but usually with lower cost and better liquidity.

EU: The European Union; a political and monetary union comprising 28 European nations and more than 500 million people.

EV: Electric vehicle.

Fiat currency: "Paper" money decreed by government regulation, without base in a commodity such as gold.

Fiscal policy: Government policy to regulate public taxation and spending levels in order to promote economic growth and welfare.

FTSE: Financial Times Stock Exchange; refers here to FTSE International Ltd, a British provider of stock indexes and other financial data services owned by the London Stock Exchange.

FX: Foreign exchange market; financial term for currency trading.

GDP: Gross Domestic Product; a measurement of the total output in the national economy.

GHG: Greenhouse gas; air molecules in the atmosphere such as water vapour, carbon dioxide, ozone, nitrous oxide, methane and others that cause the earth to warm.

GIC: The Government of Singapore Investment Corporation Pte Ltd; the sovereign wealth fund of Singapore investing most of the country's public savings and pensions funds.

GMO: Genetically Modified Organism; often used in reference to food crops and animals that have been genetically altered in laboratories.

Great Recession: This event started in the US in December 2007 and lasted till the stock market revival in March 2009, causing economic contraction and unemployment throughout most of the world.

Hedge fund: Mutual fund that uses derivatives to enhance risk as well as return; large initial investment can be difficult to redeem.

IEA: International Energy Agency; Paris-based agency under the auspices of the OECD.

IPCC: The Intergovernmental Panel on Climate Change; a scientific research body under the auspices of the UN.

IQ: Intelligence Quotient; a standardised test score to indicate a person's intelligence.

iShares: A range of ETFs managed by BlackRock, the world's largest asset manager.

IUCN: International Union for Conservation of Nature; an international organisation based in Switzerland and working for nature conservation and sustainable use of resources.

LTA: Land Transport Authority; a statutory board under the Government of Singapore.

Macroeconomics: Economics that deals with the larger national and international concepts such as national income, trade, employment, savings and interest rates.

MAS: Monetary Authority of Singapore; the central bank of Singapore. MAS conducts monetary policy, issues currency, supervises banks and manages the official foreign reserves in order to promote sustained non-inflationary economic growth.

MNC: Multinational Corporation.

Monetary policy: The policy of central banks to control the money supply and interest rates in order to promote growth and full employment in the economy.

MSCI: Morgan Stanley Capital International (MSCI Inc); a New York-based provider of stock market indexes and other financial analysis tools.

Mutual fund: A collective fund of pooled investments actively managed by professional managers according to the terms set out in a prospectus.

MWp: Megawatt-peak; a measure of peak capacity for a solar power panel or system.

NASA: National Aeronautics and Space Administration; the American governmental space agency.

NASDAQ: Second only to the NYSE as the largest stock exchange in the world; based in New York; many technology companies list here.

NAV: Net Asset Value; the value of all assets minus liabilities in a mutual fund. Divide this by number of shares to get NAV per share.

NGO: Non-Governmental Organisation; a non-profit organisation set up and funded by ordinary citizens.

NYSE: The New York Stock Exchange; the big board of American listed companies and by far the largest exchange in the world by capitalisation.

OECD: Organisation for Economic Co-operation and Development; Paris-based forum that currently includes 35 of the most developed countries.

p.a.: Per annum; usually used for interest or yield paid or calculated over one year.

PAP: People's Action Party; the ruling political party of Singapore.

Paris climate accord: International agreement from December 2015 to limit global warming below 2°C by 2100; all countries except the US have signed on.

PV: Photovoltaic; a solar energy technology using solar panels made of semiconductor cells to generate electricity.

QE: Quantitative easing; the policy of central banks to buy government bonds and thereby expand the money supply, i.e. to "print money".

SDGs: Sustainable Development Goals; a set of 17 goals identified by the UN ranging from fighting poverty and injustice to promoting education and responsible production.

REDD: Reducing emissions from deforestation and degradation; a UN-sponsored scheme to reward sound forest management in developing countries.

REIT: Real estate investment trust; a trust investing in a specified range of properties; many are publicly listed companies and shares can be traded on a stock exchange by retail investors.

RI: Responsible Investment; another term for ethical investing.

RSPB: Royal Society for the Protection of Birds; UK-based NGO.

S&P 500: An index tracking 500 major companies listed on the NYSE as well as NASDAQ; considered the best indicator of the performance of American listed companies.

SEB: Sharing Economy Business; a new business model built on trust, internet access and sharing of resources such as homes, vehicles, peer-to-peer lending, etc.

SGX: Singapore Exchange Ltd; a listed company in Singapore functioning as an exchange for stocks, bonds, derivatives and other securities products.

SPDR funds: Standard & Poor's Depositary Receipts, pronounced "spider"; a range of ETFs managed by State Street Global Advisors.

SRI: Sustainable Responsible Investing; also sometimes Socially Responsible Investing or Sustainable Responsible Impact investing.

STI: Straits Times Index; benchmark index for Singapore's stock market; tracks 30 large-capitalisation component stocks as calculated by Singapore Press Holdings, SGX and FTSE Group.

Temasek: Often used in short form for Temasek Holdings Pte Ltd; an investment company wholly owned by the Singapore government and regarded as a national wealth fund.

UN: United Nations.

VC: Venture capital or venture capitalist; a type of private equity provided by wealthy individuals to fund early-stage companies with high growth potential.

WTO: World Trade Organisation; formed in 1994 to replace the 1948 GATT (General Agreement on Tariffs and Trade).

WWF: World Wide Fund for Nature; an international NGO working for biodiversity conservation and the reduction of humanity's footprint on the environment.

Persons referred to

Aburdene, Patricia. Born 1947. American bestselling author and public speaker; specialises in issues such as the future, business trends and women in business.

Andersen, Hans Christian. 1805–1875. Danish author of poems, novels and travel stories but best known for his fairy tales translated into more than 125 languages and dramatised countless times.

Armstrong, Fraser A. Born 1951. British scientist and author; professor of chemistry at the University of Oxford.

Bales, Kevin B. Born 1952. UK-based American academic and human rights activist; co-founder of Free the Slaves; currently professor of contemporary slavery at the University of Nottingham.

Bezos, Jeffrey P. ("Jeff"). Born 1964. American businessman; founder, chairman and CEO of Amazon.com Inc; with assets in excess of US$100 billion currently the richest man in the world.

Bloomberg, Michael R. Born 1942. American media tycoon, businessman and philanthropist; mayor of New York City 2002–2013.

Blundell, Katherine. British scientist and author; professor of astrophysics at the University of Oxford.

Branson, Richard C.N. Born 1950. British billionaire businessman with interests in music, publishing, aviation, transport, telecommunications, healthcare, hotels, technology, etc., under the Virgin brand.

Brundtland, Gro H. Born 1939. Norwegian physician and politician; former prime minister of Norway; known for having chaired the Brundtland Commission on sustainable development.

Buffett, Warren E. Born 1930. American investor and philanthropist; the guru and inspiration to countless other value investors.

Carson, Rachel L. 1907–1964. American biologist, conservationist and award-winning writer; author of *Silent Spring* (1962) about the damage caused by synthetic pesticides such as DDT.

Carter, James E. ("Jimmy"). Born 1924. 39th President of the United States (Democrat) 1977–1981.

Cash, John R. ("Johnny"). 1932–2003. American guitar player, singer, song-writer and actor; one of the bestselling country musicians of all time.

Casse, Thorkil. Danish academic and researcher; a specialist in environmental economics and forest management; currently associate professor at Roskilde University, Denmark.

Clinton, William J. ("Bill"). Born 1946. 42nd President of the United States (Democrat) 1993–2001.

Confucius. 551 BC–479 BC. Chinese philosopher and teacher; founder of Confucianism teaching correctness, justice and strong family loyalty.

Cook, James. 1728–1779. British navy captain; a hugely influential navigator and explorer; covered all the Seven Seas in three major voyages.

Costanza, Robert. Born 1950. American ecological economist and sustainability scientist; currently professor of public policy at the Australian National University.

Daly, Herman E. Born 1938. American economist, professor at the University of Maryland specialising in ecological economics.

Diamond, Jared M. Born 1937. American academic, ecologist and bestselling author; currently professor of geology at the University of California, LA.

Domini, Amy. Born 1950. American investment manager, author and philanthropist; CEO of Domini Impact Investments; also founder of the Domini 400 Social Index.

Duterte, Rodrigo R. Born 1945. Philippine lawyer and politician; President of the Philippines since 2016.

Ehrlich, Paul R. Born 1932. American biologist and ecologist with somewhat alarmist views, especially about population growth; currently professor at Stanford University.

Faber, Marc. Born 1946. Thailand-based Swiss investor, financial analyst and media commentator; known for his *Gloom, Boom & Doom* online report.

Feigenbaum, Cliff. American businessman and writer; since 1992 founder and owner of e-journal *GreenMoney Journal* and GreenMoney.com.

Flannery, Timothy F. ("Tim"). Born 1956. Australian zoologist, environmentalist, climate change activist and author; professorial fellow at the University of Melbourne; named Australian of the Year 2007.

Fonda, Jane S. Born 1937. American actress, fashion model and fitness guru; known for her political activism and liberal views.

Ford, Henry. 1863–1947. American business mogul; founded the Ford Motor Company and pioneered car mass production.

Forooha, Rana. Born 1970. American journalist and writer; associate editor with the *Financial Times* and economic analyst with CNN.

Francesch-Huidobro, Maria. Spanish academic with a PhD in politics and public administration; based in Hong Kong as a consultant with Konrad Adenauer Stiftung.

Galbraith, John Kenneth. 1908–2006. Canadian-American economist; one of the most influential academics and economic policy advisers during the 20th century with a strong liberal bias.

Gates, William H. ("Bill"). Born 1955. American businessman and philanthropist; co-founder of Microsoft and one of the world's richest people.

Geh Min. Born 1953. Singaporean ophthalmologist and award-winning environmentalist; former nominated member of parliament.

Goldacre, Ben M. Born 1974. British doctor and researcher; writes the Bad Science column for *The Guardian*, critical of alternative medicine and the pharmaceutical industry.

Goodall, Jane M. Born 1934. British primatologist, anthropologist and nature conservationist; founder of the Jane Goodall Institute and the Roots and Shoots programme.

Grantham, Jeremy. Born 1938. American-based British investor and fund manager; an expert in analysing "bubbles" in the economy and the environment.

Gupta, Piyush. Born 1960. Singapore-based Indian banker; currently CEO of DBS Group; named 2014 Singapore Business Leader of the Year by CNBC.

Hawking, Stephen W. 1942–2018. British scientist, author and public speaker; an expert in quantum physics, gravity and black holes.

Helliwell, John F. Born 1937. Canadian economist, researcher and academic; professor emeritus at the University of British Columbia; known for his work in the economics of well-being and happiness.

Helm, Dieter R. Born 1956. British economist specialising in energy and environmental issues; professor at the University of Oxford and chair of the Natural Capital Committee.

Hickel, Jason. UK-based South African academic and author; currently research fellow at the Department of Anthropology at the London School of Economics; writes regularly for the *Guardian* and *Al Jazeera*.

Hoover, Herbert C. 1874–1964. 31st President of the United States (Republican) 1929–1933.

Humes, Edward. Born 1957. American writer, teacher, public speaker and Pulitzer Prize-winning author based in southern California.

Jones, Garett. Born 1970. American economist and author; studies macroeconomic concepts and intelligence in relation to productivity; associate professor at George Mason University.

Juniper, Tony. Born 1960. British academic and conservationist; former director of Friends of the Earth; senior associate at the University of Cambridge.

Khan IV, Aga. Born 1936. British-Arabic royal prince, imam and wealthy businessman; works to reduce poverty and promote secular pluralism, women's education and environmental protection.

Klare, Michael T. Born 1942. American academic and writer; currently professor at Hampshire College, Massachusetts; author of many books dealing with resource depletion and security issues.

Klein, Naomi. Born 1970. Award-winning Canadian writer and filmmaker taking neoliberal economics and environmentally damaging capitalism to task.

Koch brothers; Charles (born 1935) and David (born 1940). American billionaire business tycoons and owners of the Koch Industries Inc industrial empire; active in politics lobbying for conservative causes.

Lambertini, Marco. Born 1958. Italian scientist, author and nature conservationist; since 2014 Director General of WWF International.

Leahy, Patrick J. Born 1940. American politician; has served in the Senate (Democrat from Vermont) since 1975.

Lehrer, Thomas, A. ("Tom"). Born 1928. American mathematics professor and entertainer, now retired; composed and performed a number of satirical songs during the 1960s.

Lynn, Richard. Born 1930. English psychologist, academic and writer; best known for his work on intelligence.

Macdonald, David W. Born 1951. British biologist and conservationist; specialist in large carnivore mammals; professor at Oxford University; award-winning writer and film-maker.

MacKinnon, James B. Born 1970. Canadian writer, journalist and award-winning author; often covering environmental, food and outdoor themes.

Mason, Paul. Born 1960. British teacher, journalist, broadcaster and bestselling author with a left-leaning social democratic platform.

Mitchell, Andrew. British ecologist and environmentalist; founder director of Global Canopy as well as founder and CEO of Equilibrium Futures.

Moffitt, Lena. American environmentalist; currently senior director of the Sierra Club's Our Wild America campaign.

Morris, Desmond J. Born 1928. British zoologist, painter, broadcaster and author; famous for writing *The Naked Ape* (1967).

Moskovitz, Dustin A. Born 1984. American internet entrepreneur and philanthropist; made his billions as co-founder of Facebook.

Murdoch, Rupert K. Born 1931. American media tycoon; former Australian; executive chairman of his holding company News Corp and acting chairman of Fox News.

Musk, Elon R. Born 1971. South African, Canadian and American engineer, inventor and business tycoon; CEO of SpaceX and Tesla Inc.

Myers, Norman. Born 1934. British environmentalist and writer; specialises in studies of biodiversity and climate refugees; has provided advice to the UN, the World Bank and various academic institutions.

Nixon, Richard M. 1913–1994. 37th President of the United States (Republican) 1969–1974.

Nowak, Tom M. American financial adviser; founder and principal of Quantum Financial Planning.

Obomsawin, Alanis. Born 1932. Canadian of Native American decent; award-winning documentary film-maker.

Pennells, Sarah. British journalist, blogger, broadcaster and author; specialises in financial advice for women.

Ponting, Clive S. Born 1946. British historian; former civil servant and author of many books, often challenging the official version of events.

Ponzi, Charles. 1882–1949. Italian-born businessman based in the U.S.; gave name to the financial swindle scheme where you pay investors huge "dividends" with money from new investors, until the money flow stops and the investors lose their deposits.

Pye-Smith, Charlie. Born 1951. British writer and broadcaster; specialises in issues relating to agriculture, nature conservation and the environment.

Razzouk, Assaad W. Born 1964. Lebanese-British banker and businessman; currently CEO of Sindicatum Sustainable Resources, London.

Reagan, Ronald W. 1911–2004. 40th President of the United States (Republican) 1981–1989.

Rogers, James B. ("Jim"). Born 1942. Singapore-based American investor and author with a libertarian and contrarian outlook.

Roggeveen, Jacob. 1659–1729. Dutch explorer who sailed via the Falkland Islands west across the Pacific Ocean to Indonesia.

Sanders, Bernie. Born 1941. American politician; currently senator representing Vermont, a self-confessed socialist; serious contender for the Democratic Party presidential primary elections in 2016.

Sandor, Richard L. Born 1942. American entrepreneur and award-winning economist with expertise in derivatives trading and environmental finance; currently Chairman and CEO of Environmental Financial Products LLT.

Seba, Tony. American businessman, academic, bestselling author and keynote speaker; currently lecturer at Stanford University; famous for predicting the demise of oil and the dawn of clean energy and transport.

Stein, Jill E. Born 1950. American medical doctor and politician; presidential candidate for the Green Party in 2012 and 2016.

Stern, Nicholas H. Born 1946. British academic and economist; professor at the London School of Economics; main author of the 2006 *Stern Review* about the cost of climate change.

Stoltenberg, Jens. Born 1959. Norwegian politician; prime minister of Norway from 2000 to 2001 and again from 2005 to 2013; currently Secretary General of NATO.

Strange, Daniel K. Born 1988. Danish language and philosophy academic; currently teaches high school in Greenland; also my son.

Taylor, John B. Born 1946. American economist; former under-secretary of the Treasury, currently professor at Stanford University; influential in developing various macroeconomic models, most noticeably the Taylor Rule.

Tesla, Nikola. 1856–1943. Serbian-American electrical engineer and inventor; pioneered the use of alternating current electricity and foresaw the use of wireless technology.

Trump, Donald J. Born 1946. 45th President of the United States (Republican) from 2017.

Turner, Robert E. ("Ted"). Born 1938. American entrepreneur and media mogul; founder of the CNN 24-hour cable news TV station; environmentalist, philanthropist and major land-owner.

Underwood, Carrie M. Born 1983. Grammy Award-winning and bestselling American country singer, songwriter and actress.

Ustinov, Peter A. 1921–2004. Award-winning British actor, director, filmmaker, writer and TV personality.

Watson, Robert T. Born 1948. British scientist; an expert on atmospheric and global warming studies; director at the University of East Anglia.

Weyler, Rex. Born 1947. American-Canadian environmentalist and author; co-founder of Greenpeace International; currently freelance writer, journalist and broadcaster.

Wicherts, Jelte M. Born 1976. Dutch psychologist and researcher; professor at Tilburg University.

Yellen, Janet L. Born 1946. American economist; chair of the Federal Reserve from 2014 to 2018.

References

Major works used when preparing this book

Aburdene, Patricia. 2012. *Conscious Money: Living, Creating, and Investing with Your Values for a Sustainable New Prosperity.* New York: Simon & Schuster.

Armstrong, Fraser & Blundell, Katherine. 2007. *Energy... Beyond Oil.* Oxford: Oxford University Press.

Brassington, Mark. 2008. *How to Go Carbon Neutral.* Oxford: How To Books.

Diamond, Jared. 2011. *Collapse: How Societies Choose to Fail or Succeed.* London: Penguin Books.

Flannery, Tim. 2009. *NOW or NEVER: Why We Must Act Now to End Climate Change and Create a Sustainable Future.* New York: Atlantic Monthly Press.

Flannery, Tim. 2012. *Here on Earth: A Twin Biography of the Planet and the Human Race.* London: Penguin Books.

Foroohar, Rana. 2016. *Makers and Takers: How Wall Street Destroyed Main Street.* New York: Crown Publishing Group.

Francesch-Huidobro, Maria. 2008. *Governance, Politics and the Environment: A Singapore Study.* Singapore: Institute of Southeast Asian Studies.

Goldacre, Ben. 2008. *Bad Science.* London: HarperCollins.

Helm, Dieter. 2015. *Natural Capital: Valuing the Planet.* London: Yale University Press.

Humes, Edward. 2009. *Eco Barons.* New York: HarperCollins.

Jones, Garett. 2016. *Hive Mind.* California: Stanford University Press.

Juniper, Tony. 2013. *What Has Nature Ever Done for Us? How Money Really Does Grow On Trees.* London: Profile Books.

Klare, Michael T. 2012. *The Race for What's Left: The Global Scramble for the World's Last Resources.* New York: Metropolitan Books.

Klein, Naomi. 2014. *This Changes Everything: Capitalism vs. The Climate.* London: Penguin Books.

MacKinnon, James B. 2013. *The Once and Future World: Nature As It Was, As It Is, As It Could Be.* New York: Houghton Mifflin Harcourt.

Mason, P. 2015. *Postcapitalism: A Guide to Our Future.* London: Penguin Books.

Myers, Norman. 1979. *The Sinking Ark: A New Look at the Problem of Disappearing Species.* Oxford: Pergamon Press.

Nowak, Tom. 2012. *Low Fee Socially Responsible Investing: Investing in Your Worldview on Your Terms.* Illinois: Quantum Financial Planning.

Pennells, Sarah. 2009. *Green Money: How to Save and Invest Ethically.* London: A&C Black.

Ponting, Clive. 2007. *A New Green History of the World: The Environment and the Collapse of Great Civilisation.* London: Random House.

Pye-Smith, Charlie. 2002. *The Subsidy Scandal: How Your Government Wastes Your Money to Wreck Your Environment.* London: Earthscan Publications.

Strange, Morten. 2016. *Be Financially Free: How to Become Salary Independent in Today's Economy.* Singapore: Marshall Cavendish Editions.

Useful websites

For general definition of financial terms and videos I find this site very fun and useful: http://www.investopedia.com/

Specifically about ethical investing, you can try to start off with the US SIF, The Forum for Sustainable and Responsible Investment and their site: https://www.ussif.org

This organisation is a member of the Global Sustainable Investment Alliance: http://www.gsi-alliance.org/

The UK of course also has its own Sustainable Investment and Finance Association (UK SIF): http://uksif.org/
… as well as an Ethical Investment Association (EIA): http://ethicalinvestment.org.uk/

For the US, there is the Social Funds site with thousands of pages on SRI: http://www.socialfunds.com/

More targeting institutional investors and exchanges, the Environmental Financial Products site based in the US has some more technical resources and links: http://www.envifi.com/

Environmental Finance is UK-based and has a very comprehensive website as well as a quarterly magazine: https://www.environmental-finance.com/

Although again somewhat UK-centred in focus, this site has a lot of useful info on both SRI and more general environmental issues: http://blueandgreentomorrow.com

In Singapore, the Eco-Business news site prides itself on taking an environmental view to business development and finance: http://www.eco-business.com/

For possible solutions, try to check out this site building on the Steady State Economy idea: https://steadystate.org/

And finally my personal favourite, with easy-to-adopt practical solutions: http://simplerway.org/

MORTEN STRANGE (born 1952, Denmark) is a Singapore-based IBF-certified independent financial analyst. Since becoming salary-independent and retiring at the age of 33, he has pursued his interests in economics and finance, writing, photography, and environmental conservation. He is the author of *Be Financially Free: How to Become Salary Independent in Today's Economy* (2016, Marshall Cavendish Editions).

"*Be Financially Free* by 'citizen economist' Morten Strange is not just a good book, it is a fantastic piece of entertainment, common sense economics, and wisdom about life, and how to achieve financial independence, and to 'live', as Pablo Picasso said, 'as a poor man with lots of money'. Strange will not win a Nobel Prize with *Be Financially Free*, but he has my respect for having written a highly readable, funny and cynical financial essay, which actually makes sense."

— DR MARC FABER
Financial analyst, international fund manager,
and publisher of the *Gloom Boom & Doom Report*